D0383160

The Story of the Meininger

Books of the Theatre Series

H. D. Albright, General Editor

Number 4   *August 1963*

A Rare Books of the Theatre project of the
American Educational Theatre Association

MAX GRUBE'S

"The Story of the Meininger"

translated by
Ann Marie Koller

Edited by Wendell Cole

UNIVERSITY OF MIAMI PRESS
CORAL GABLES, FLORIDA 33146

Printed in the United States of America
PARKER PRINTING, CORAL GABLES, FLORIDA

CONTENTS

FOREWORD

As the fourth volume in the Books of the Theatre Series — jointly sponsored by the American Educational Theatre Association and the University of Miami Press — the editors are pleased to offer, for the first time in English, *The Story of the Meininger,* by Max Grube. Originally published as *Geshichte der Meininger* in 1926, the book has been translated and published here with the permission of Deutsche Verlags-Anstalt, Stuttgart, the original publishers.

Several of the photographs and prints from the German edition are reproduced in the present volume; others are presented by arrangement with the Meininger Museum and the Cologne Theatre Museum. In each case specific credits are given in the captions accompanying the several plates.

Two of the three tables appearing in *Geschichte der Meininger* are duplicated in an appendix to the present edition. A few minor discrepancies found in the original tables could not be satisfactorily checked against the Meininger records, and they have been reproduced as they appeared in 1926.

Special acknowledgement for support and assistance on *The Story of the Meininger* is due to the Rare Books Project of the American Educational Theatre Association, of which David G. Schaal is the current Chairman.

H. D. ALBRIGHT
General Editor

INTRODUCTION

Most American theatre students are aware that after Henry Irving attended the Meininger performances in London in 1881, he modeled his famous Lyceum Shakespearean productions on what he had seen; that when Constantin Stanislavski visited a Meininger rehearsal in Moscow in 1885, he resolved to imitate the autocratic directing methods of Ludwig Chronegk; and that in Brussels in 1888 André Antoine was overwhelmed by the extraordinary realism in the Meininger crowd scenes.

If the Duke of Saxe-Meiningen did not inaugurate twentieth-century stagecraft himself, he may be considered the most significant influence on those directors who did. He made every important European director conscious that scenery must be designed to fit the movements of actors; that costumes, properties, and lighting must contribute to the creation of the mood and atmosphere of the stage picture; and that no detail of interpretation or stage business was so small that it was not worth careful research, planning, and rehearsal. World-renowned for their crowd scenes, his productions were triumphs of ensemble playing. As Max Grube reminds us, Duke Georg II established the supremacy in the modern theatre of the Régisseur—the director who unifies the production through his complete control of every moment of the actor's interpretation and movements, and every detail of setting, lighting, costuming, and make-up.

Very little has been translated from the many descriptions in German of the Meininger productions. Even though the best known of these accounts is Grube's *Geschichte der Meininger,* it, too, has never appeared in an English translation. In his Preface Grube tells us, "I believe that I am duly qualified to write the story of the Meininger." He was, indeed, in an especially advantageous situation to do so, for he had not only appeared in the first guest performances of the Meininger in Berlin in 1874 when he was twenty years old, but he had spent seventeen seasons from 1872 to 1888 as an actor in the company of Duke Georg.

Born in Dorpat, Germany, in 1854, Grube attended school in Berlin, and at the age of eighteen obtained his first position as a professional actor with the Meiningen Court Theatre. In his book he refers particularly to his experiences with the Meininger while playing Talbot in *The Maid of Orleans* and the title part in Byron's *Marino Faliero,* but he was equally well-known in such Shakespearean roles as Shylock, Iago, Lear, Malvolio, and Richard III, and as Franz Moor in Schiller's *The Robbers* and Mephistopheles in Goethe's *Faust*. In 1888 he left the Meininger to accept a position as an actor at the Royal Playhouse in Berlin, but occasionally returned to Meiningen for guest appearances. On becoming the principal director of the Berlin Royal Playhouse in 1890, he obtained an opportunity to introduce many of the production methods of Duke Georg into a company notorious for its old-fashioned stagecraft. When the Meiningen Court Theatre was rebuilt by the Duke after the destructive fire of 1908, Grube was asked to return to Meiningen as Intendant. There he remained in the office once held by the famed Ludwig Chronegk until 1913, when he left to join the company at the Hamburg Playhouse. After five very successful seasons at Hamburg, he returned once more to Meiningen in 1918 to play such character roles as Nathan the Wise.

During his long and strenuous career as an actor and director, he found time to write many poems, several plays, a biography of the great German actor Adalbert Matkowsky, an edition of Seydelmann's *Acting Notebooks,* two books of theatre history, and two volumes of his memoirs. His *Story of the Meininger,* written when he was more than seventy years old and living in retirement in Meiningen, has remained the basic work on the staging methods of Duke Georg. While this book is our best single source for information on the Meininger, we cannot regard it as a scholarly study. Grube remarks about his namesake Karl Grube (who had written *Die Meininger,* a brief record of his experiences as an actor with the Duke's company): "He chats delightfully, but lacks thoroughness." We can make the same comment on Max Grube and his *Story of the Meininger.* In any case, the present translation attempts to preserve much of Grube's informal and colloquial style. First published in 1926, *Geschichte der Meininger* appeared on the one-hundredth anniversary of the Duke's birth.

Before his death at Meiningen on December 25, 1934, Grube had lived to see the German stage, once ruled by the "authentic antiquarianism" of the Meininger, fall first under the influence of impressionism before World War I, next under the sway of expressionism in the early twenties, and finally under the dominance of a group of egocentric directors each of whom insisted upon stamping his personal style on every production. In his Preface Grube recognizes that by 1926 the methods of the Meininger no longer prevailed in the German theatre.

He could assume that his readers in 1926 were familiar with much German political and theatrical history which is obscure to us today. It is therefore appropriate to provide in this Introduction some additional information about the theatrical history of Meiningen and the triumvirate who "commanded the destinies of the Meininger": Duke Georg II of Saxe-Meiningen; his wife Helene, Baroness von Heldburg; and the Court Theatre Intendant, Ludwig Chronegk.

The establishment of the Meiningen Court Theatre is commemorated as having occurred on September 6, 1781 when a group of commoners performed a comic opera, *The Hunt* (by Weisse with music by Hiller), in a room in Castle Elizabethenburg. Duke Karl, the ruler of Meiningen at that time, had become interested in theatre and music during his student days at Strasbourg. Five years earlier in 1776, the year of the first performance in Germany of Klinger's *Sturm und Drang,* which gave its name to a literary era, Duke Karl had built a stage in his castle at Meiningen. There members of the ducal family and court society had appeared as actors under the direction of the ducal librarian, Reinwald, a friend of Schiller and later his brother-in-law. Some of the plays performed by these titled amateurs are listed by Grube. After 1781 the castle stage was used by the so-called Commoner's Society, composed of young officials, court musicians, and their families. According to Grube the date of the first professional performance in Meiningen was 1785. By the early nineteenth century, the Commoner's Society was no longer active, but various travelling troupes gave performances in the castle, at the riding school, and at the Saxon Court Inn.

During 1829 stock shares for the construction of a Court Theatre were sold under the sponsorship of Duke Bernhard II, the father of Georg II. As the result of a successful stock sale, a building was erected in 1829-31 on Bernhard Street in Meiningen from plans by the Braunschweig architect, Othmer. The theatre was inaugurated on Duke Bernhard's birthday in 1831 with a performance of the opera *Fra Diavolo.* This building, designed in a classic-revival style with a facade decorated with red sandstone pillars crowned by a Greek pediment, contained not only the auditorium and stage house but also an assembly hall for balls, banquets, and other festive occasions. It was in this building that Duke Georg established his Meiningen company, and from there the Meininger set forth on their guest tours. After the success of the Meininger tours in the seventies, the stage house area was enlarged to provide for more elaborate scenic effects. On March 5, 1908, after more than 76 years of service, the Court Theatre was destroyed by fire. The theatre which stands today in Meiningen was erected by Duke Georg and opened on his father's birthday in 1909.

Georg II, the "Theatre Duke," was born on April 2, 1826, the only child of Duke Bernhard II until the birth of a sister when Georg was in his teens. Georg's first teachers were a theologian, Johannes Klug, and the court artist, Paul Schellhorn. The former seems to have instilled in Georg a love of nature, the latter a love of art. When Georg was nine his education was taken over by Professor Moritz Seebeck. At that time his instruction in art was continued by the historical painter, Wilhelm Lindenschmitt, who had painted murals at Castle Landsberg. In 1843 Captain Eduard von Reitzenstein of the Royal Saxon Army was assigned as the military tutor of the young prince, and the following year, accompanied by Captain Reitzenstein and Professor Seebeck, Georg entered the University of Bonn to study law, political economy, and history. His major interests, however, seem to have been art and military science.

During the two and a half years when he was a student at Bonn, he made trips to Paris and Dresden and, for one semester, attended the

University of Leipzig, where he became acquainted with the composer Felix Mendelssohn. Upon leaving the University of Bonn, he went to Berlin as First Lieutenant in the Royal Guards. At the court of King Friedrich Wilhelm IV, Georg met the artists Peter von Cornelius and Wilhelm Kaulbach, continuing under their guidance his drawing and painting and also devoting himself to a study of classical music.

Since Grube mentions various members of the ducal family without always identifying them clearly for us, a simplified family tree of the Dukes of Saxe-Meiningen may be helpful.

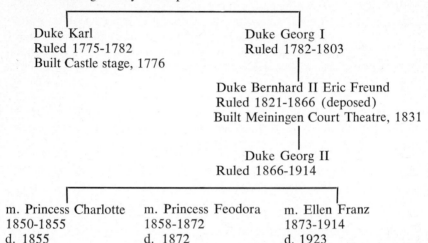

Duke Karl
Ruled 1775-1782
Built Castle stage, 1776

Duke Georg I
Ruled 1782-1803

Duke Bernhard II Eric Freund
Ruled 1821-1866 (deposed)
Built Meiningen Court Theatre, 1831

Duke Georg II
Ruled 1866-1914

m. Princess Charlotte
1850-1855
d. 1855

m. Princess Feodora
1858-1872
d. 1872

m. Ellen Franz
1873-1914
d. 1923

During the political revolts of March, 1848, Prince Georg was ordered by his father to return to Meiningen. There in May, 1850, he married Princess Charlotte, the daughter of Prince Albrecht of Prussia. In 1855, after the birth of their three children, Princess Charlotte died at the age of twenty-four. The Prince turned for consolation to his art and music and in 1855-56 travelled in Italy with the painter Andreas Müller. After his return to Meiningen in 1858 he married Princess Feodora of Hohenlohe-Langenburg.

At this time Prussia was assuming a dominant position among the German states under the leadership of Wilhelm I and his prime minister Bismarck. Because of Prussia's attitude towards the smaller states, Duke Bernhard feared that his own sovereignty was endangered. He turned to Austria for support, and in June, 1866, he was one of the German Princes who voted in the National Assembly for a military pact with Austria against Prussia. As a result, in September, 1866, Prussia sent two battalions to occupy Meiningen and to force the abdication of Duke Bernhard in favor of his son, Prince Georg, who was known to be sympathetic towards the unification of Germany. Thus through these rather special circumstances Georg became the ruler of Meiningen at the age of forty. As the Duke of Saxe-Meiningen, he served in the Franco-Prussian War of 1870, and was present in the Hall of Mirrors at Versailles on the historic occasion in January 1871 when Wilhelm I, the King of Prussia, was proclaimed the Emperor of Germany.

As Grube points out, Georg's interest in the Meiningen Court Theatre had begun at least as early as 1849, shortly after his return from Berlin. We should not forget that during the years when he was so actively engaged in the productions of the Meininger, he was also directing the affairs of state in his country. As a typical "enlightened monarch" of the late nineteenth century, he liberalized the land-owning laws (1867), promoted trade agreements and tariff reform (1869, 1872), supported new penal codes (1871, 1876), and encouraged the establishment of technical schools and welfare institutions and the building of churches and hospitals. By the opening years of the twentieth century, Meiningen, like the other progressive German states of that period, was offering housing loans, constructing public utilities, and providing various welfare services.

Princess Feodora, who had become the mother of two sons by the Duke, died in 1872, leaving Georg a widower once more after nearly fourteen years of his second marriage. In his sorrow he devoted even more time to the productions of the Court Theatre. At rehearsals and in the home of Intendant von Bodenstedt he became acquainted with the leading actress of the company, Ellen Franz. Not only at the theatre but also on many social occasions, they continued to meet each other frequently. Falling in love with her, the Duke determined to propose to Fräulein Franz—and to enter into a morganatic marriage, since she was not of noble birth.

In 1872 Ellen Franz was thirty-three years old and had been with the Meiningen Company since 1867. She had been born in 1839 in Naumberg, Germany, the daughter of Dr. Hermann Franz and his wife Sarah, whose father was an English lord. Dr. Franz had met his future wife when he had gone to England as the tutor of Lord Livingstone's son. In 1847 Dr. Franz and his family moved to Berlin, where he became the co-founder and director of the Royal Commercial School. Grube tells us of Ellen's early life in Berlin, of her experiences in obtaining engagements in the theatre, and of the serious accident which prevented her from pursuing her career for two years. Just before accepting the position with the Meiningen Court Theatre, she had written to her brother Reinhold in 1866, "I am twenty-eight years old, no longer young for an unmarried girl. . . I have been bitterly disappointed in love, and I believe I can in all honesty say: I no longer look forward to any real happiness."

Ellen, who joined the Meiningen Company after acting experience at Saxe-Coburg, Oldenburg, Frankfurt-on-the-Oder, and Mannheim, had been the leading young actress at Meiningen for five years when the Duke proposed to her. As soon as the Duke announced his intentions, both his family and court society were aroused against an alliance with a woman who was not only a commoner but also an actress. Finally Ellen confided to her friend Anna Schwencke that in order to escape from the scandal which the Duke's proposal had caused, she had decided to sign a contract with a Hamburg theatre and leave Meiningen quickly without telling the Duke.

On an evening when one of Ellen's leading roles was taken for the first time by a guest star, Marie Berg, the newcomer received a tremendous ovation from the court group which opposed the Duke's marriage, and as the spectators left the theatre after the performance, they found scurrilous remarks scrawled on walls along the streets alleging that Ellen Franz had been discharged. Although a quiet wedding in England had been planned, the Duke decided to marry at once, and then announce the marriage as an accomplished fact. On March 18, 1873, Ellen secretly travelled by wagon through a blizzard to the ducal villa at Liebenstein, where the Duke had improvised a chapel. There they were married—with Ellen dressed in a black velvet costume from *Emilia Galotti,* since her wedding gown was unfinished. Pastor Wolff from the nearby village of Schweina appropriately chose as his text the famous passage from the Book of Ruth, "Whither thou goest, I shall go." Ludwig Chronegk and a lady-in-waiting were the only witnesses. On the same day Ellen was raised to the nobility as Helene, Baroness von Heldburg. By the time news of their marriage was released, the bridal couple was already on the way to the Duke's Villa Carlotta on Lake Como. Their marriage was to be an apparently ideally happy one of more than forty years.

The painting by the eminent Munich artist Franz von Lenbach catches the vivacious charm of this talented woman. Amanda Lindner, who made a great sensation at the age of seventeen in the role of Joan of Arc in the Meininger production of Schiller's *The Maid of Orleans,* said of Ellen Franz, "The Baroness was an ideal taskmistress, with perseverance, mildness, and patience." According to Fräulein Lindner, "the ducal couple was always full of love and goodness" at the rehearsals of *The Maid of Orleans.* After the play opened in Berlin with unprecedented success, the Baroness wrote to her "repeatedly, always full of motherly goodness and solicitude." During the guest tours both Georg and his wife remained in Meininger, where he carried on his duties as ruler. Between 1874 and 1890 the Duke saw only three performances of his company when it was on tour. After the end of the guest tours in 1890, the royal couple continued to take an active interest in the Meininger productions, although in the years immediately preceding the Duke's death at the age of eighty-eight in 1914, they spent much time away from Meiningen.

For the next nine years after his death, the Baroness resided in a small house in Meiningen, visited by numerous German theatre people who came to do honor to the woman whose husband had played such a significant role in the late nineteenth-century theatre. Before her death in 1923 she assembled a volume of correspondence and memoirs published in 1933 as *Fifty Years of Success and Sorrow.* One of the Duke's final requests was that he be interred in the Meiningen cemetery rather than in the ducal crypt in order that his wife might be buried beside him.

The third member of the "governing trinity" of the Meininger was Ludwig Chronegk who, as Grube tells us, came to the Meiningen Court Theatre in 1866 as a comic actor. In 1871, to the surprise of those members of the company who thought of him only as a comedian, the Duke appointed him Régisseur and Intendant. It was on Chronegk's advice and under his leadership that the world-famous guest tours of the Meininger were undertaken. Chronegk had been born in 1837 in Brandenburg-on-the-Havel; he attended secondary school in Berlin and Potsdam, and as a young man spent several years in Paris. Trained as a singing comedian by Karl Görner, he made his debut under this director in 1856 at Kroll's Theatre in Berlin. He appeared in several other Berlin theatres, at the Thalia in Hamburg, and at municipal theatres in Breslau, Leipzig, and Budapest, specializing in the humorous characters of Shakespeare. He was thirty-four years old when he became the director of the Meiningen Theatre. Grube describes the misgivings of other members of the company when this young comedian was selected by the Duke for such an important post. By 1874 he was so involved in managing the theatre that he had to give up his own acting career with the Meininger, although during the summers in the eighties he made several appearances as a singing comedian in other German theatres.

In addition to directing the Meininger productions under the guidance of the Duke, he edited the prompt scripts of twenty-eight of the plays and published them as *The Repertory of the Saxe-Meiningen Court Theatre, Official Edition*. He had a reputation as a thorough-going tyrant in the theatre. Probably the most famous account of his methods is that of Constantin Stanislavski in *My Life in Art*. Stanislavski describes Chronegk at a rehearsal giving the signal for its beginning by ringing a large bell. The company watched in absolute silence until he rang the bell again in order to make comments on the scene just played. "The restraint and cold-bloodedness of Chronegk were to my taste," wrote Stanislavski, "and I wanted to imitate him. With time I also became a despotic stage director." That Chronegk obtained the respect of his actors in spite of such methods and that he could be both considerate and thoughtful is affirmed by Grube. The high regard in which he was held by the Duke and Ellen Franz is indicated in Grube's account. Yet how much of the success of the Meininger was due to Chronegk and how much to the two other members of the "trinity" is never resolved by Grube. In any case, the Duke was determined not to go on with the guest tours after Chronegk's death in 1891.

Now long out of print, the *Geschichte der Meininger* is known to most English-speaking readers only through a relatively brief discussion by Lee Simonson in Part III, Chapter I, of his *The Stage is Set,* first published in 1932. At the time when Grube's book appeared in 1926, many of the methods of the Meininger seemed to belong to a remote past, for more

xvii

than twenty-five years of diverse influences had altered the theories of theatrical production. Grube is very much aware of this, as he points out in both his Preface and his concluding chapter. Were the Duke's staging methods merely the culminating point in the nineteenth-century vogue for "realistic authenticity," or did he profoundly influence every aspect of twentieth-century theatrical production? Now that almost forty more years have passed before the publication of this first English translation, we are, no doubt, in a position to evaluate the place of the Duke of Saxe-Meiningen in theatre history with even more discernment than did Max Grube. Certainly the American student will have a much better opportunity to judge for himself.

WENDELL COLE

MAX GRUBE'S

"The Story of the Meininger"

Translated by Ann Marie Koller

Artists are nothing; art alone has worth; that is to say, only that artist who promotes art as such for the benefit of mankind is worth our support. On that other artist, however, the one who approaches art with frivolity and uses it merely to delude the public—on him we should make war, to prevent him from doing harm. Now and as long as I live, my wrath is turned against, and will continue to be turned against, everything frivolous in art. Let not the man to whom God has given a talent bury it. Accordingly, I, too, shall use my small portion of artistic ability in the service of the Highest. If I regard art more highly than many others, this should not be held against me as much as against the others to whom art is less holy.

GEORG
DUKE OF SAXE-MEININGEN

From a letter to
Intendant von Stein, 1862

PREFACE

After a long, honor-crowned reign the Meininger have now finally stepped down from the throne of the stage and have had to make way for a new Lord of the Theatre Kingdom.

One? No, rather for a number of the Diadochi—for our theatre no longer knows a universally recognized method of staging suitable for all kinds of productions, such as that which the Meininger gave to the stage in their time. The speech of the Director in the Prologue to *Faust* has taken on a most "literal" meaning:

> You know, on our German stages
> Everyone tries whatever he desires.

On one hand, we have the stylized theatre, which simplifies the staging as much as possible. It removes itself as nearly as it can from reality; yet, through the use of three-dimensional scenery and of the cyclorama, it strives for the greatest approximation of reality. The effect gained by the cyclorama especially is more natural than any the illusionistic stage was ever able to produce.

Conversely, the expressionistic stage turns away completely from every imitation of naturalistic staging. It rejects Lessing's

> Let nature and art
> Be only one on the stage.

Its defenders—of whom Leopold Jessner, the Intendant of the Berliner Staatliches Schauspiel, is the most important and successful—do not wish to forget art for art's sake, the ideal of both the illusionistic and the realistic theatre. In this mode of staging, visions and phantoms can arise before the eyes of the audience and then sink down into darkness. On a black background, only suggestive effects are visible. Groups of actors, the protagonist in the foreground, are then harshly lighted by spotlights. A magical beam of light moves with the actor, following him left and right, just as in the old Chinese theatre a man with a pitch pan moved along next to the hero in order to light his face constantly.

There exist, moreover, still other methods of staging. The intimate stage has also renounced all decoration—for example, an anchor makes it clear to the audience that the scene is set in a seaport; a kitchen stool indicates that the set is a kitchen. Stylized and expressionistic staging methods overlap greatly, and both make extensive use of curtains. Nearly everyone has

• 1

also seen futuristic and cubistic designs. These styles have appeared in isolated instances or have been used mainly in cabarets, but ought not to go unmentioned here.

In comparison with all these styles of production, the art of the Meininger maintains its position only in those modern plays of social significance which do not aim at symbolism, as, for example, a play by Wedekind. And in a drawing room comedy we are still accustomed to see the rooms as fully furnished and equipped as are our own dwellings. If we accompany the characters of the comedy into a garden, then a change in scenic style becomes evident. For the garden does not resemble ours; it is stylized. We must accept a few daubs of color as bushes, jagged rags above for leaves, etc. Moreover, production methods used to treat the stage as a picture separated from the audience by a so-called Harlequin's Cloak, but now an effort is being made to do away with this frame. Some of the actors have been transferred to an arena, just as the ancient chorus took its place in the orchestra. Rising from the sides of the orchestra leading to the apron, there are steps on which the crowd and the actors can reach the stage; or by the use of levels the stage itself extends into the auditorium, and the actors enter the scene as though moving over a Japanese "flower path."

The range of modern production methods is still not exhausted by these descriptive details. Each method has found its enthusiastic eulogists; each is joyfully acclaimed and encouraged. Yet none has attained sole recognition or undivided sway. No theatre organization or staging method can boast that universal acceptance which the Meininger enjoyed in their time and which remained the standard for decades.

Here we cannot enter into the pros and cons of each of the methods in question. Each must demonstrate its own right to survive. We can oppose new artistic attempts on neither logical nor artistic grounds; each attempt raises its standards against whatever has been accepted earlier. With what justification, only the results can decide.

The staging method of the Meininger was far more different from these modern methods than they are from each other. There is certainly complete justification for the desire to find one predominant method of production for our time, so that the actor will not have to accommodate himself to constantly changing demands; yet we may rejoice that in the theatre—never known for its tranquil immobility—there has risen today a restless fermentation.

"In changing forms, art grows young again," says Heyse[1] in his beautiful, thoughtful poem, "The Banquet of the Old Men." When he has his elderly poet continue

> For favor belongs and is due to the new
> Let the aging man learn to grow old gracefully,

all the bitterness of surrender is evident, and the tone is one of resignation to an immutable law.

---

[1] Paul Heyse (1830-1914), novelist and dramatist, Nobel Prize winner (1910).

2 ·

In the Heyse poem, however, the young, laurel-crowned poet lays his newly won wreath at the feet of the old dead singer with solemn respect. Such appreciation of that which was once respected and once seemed beautiful is not evident in the character of our age; the feeling for historical value and worth seems to have been lost in the passionate struggle over new ways and goals. Nowadays, one no longer builds and develops on the past, but rather moves to crush it. In truth, poets are usually silent about a man who has been surpassed and deposed, but sometimes these same poets pour over him the vials of their ridicule and contempt.

Even the Meininger have not escaped this fate. Remarks, accompanied by condescending smiles, have frequently been made about the "Meininger sort-of-thing," remarks which have about as much relation to the real Meininger objectives as the overabundance of the Baroque has to the noble forms of the Renaissance. Indeed, our young directors have at the most seen only a few offshoots from the art of the Meininger—vigorous growth which has produced an exuberance of motley blooms, perhaps, but which gives only a weak, even false idea of the beauty and the vigor of the old plant. The last convulsive movements of a dying artistic period can give no true picture of a greatness that has been.

No knowledge exists about what the Meininger achieved, still less about what they aimed for. This is entirely natural, and no one should be blamed. The art of the director is as transitory as that of the actor. It may seem to live longer, for a production can "run" for a long time, as the theatre expression puts it. Popular pieces, as for example Ohorn's *Brothers of St. Bernard,* have played for years at the Hamburg Deutsches Theater in the same productions that Berger had devised for them; yet Berger had long since been gone from the theatre of this world. Scenery and costumes last for a long time until they fade or become threadbare, but when the spirit which breathed a soul into a dead contrivance is no longer active, the whole production becomes like a rune or a hieroglyph which only a few scholars can decipher.

Future theatre scholars should have a relatively easy time visualizing the scenic designs of our own day. Valuable sketches are now preserved in the archives of the theatre; moreover, almost every number of the numerous illustrated magazines shows photographs of stage designs and of actors in their costumes. The pictures that appeared at the time of the Meininger in the Leipzig *Illustrierte Zeitung* and in *Uber Land und Meer* can hardly be regarded as artistic, however; for in those days important artists seldom employed their skill in illustration. In addition, few of the photographs reproduce the charm of the grouping or the entire set design. The wood engravings that the magazines then employed probably would have been able to reproduce the magic which the Meininger fairly breathed —one is reminded, for example, of the beautiful landscape woodcuts of Closs—but the pictures of the Meininger productions had to be prepared quickly in order to satisfy daily requirements. They give scarcely any indication of what the art of the Meininger offered. At that time, of course, snapshots were still unknown.

Fortunately, a few scene designs from the hand of the Duke have been preserved and are offered to the public for the first time in this book. Unfortunately, the charm of color is missing here. An endless amount of writing has been done about the Meininger. They have set in motion the best pens of criticism, but this material has in part disappeared or has been so scattered that it could be assembled only with great effort. Two little books by Hans Herrig[2] and Prölss[3] are concerned with the new art of production; yet they stand too close within the frame of the contemporary period to give a definitive judgment. A gaily written little book by my namesake, Karl Grube,[4] chats delightfully, but lacks thoroughness.

In his recently published *History of Directing,*[5] Adolf Winds could not devote a great amount of space to the Meininger because of the abundance of material he was covering. They are, however, excellently characterized by his concise remarks.

The best that has been said about them can be found in Karl Frenzel's *Berlin Dramaturgy.*[6] The reviews found in this book reveal a warmth seldom apparent in this sagacious, yet cool, critic. Bulthaupt, too, in his *Dramaturgy of the Classicists*[7] gives extraordinarily valuable and remarkably brilliant descriptions, poetically perceived.

Books on the drama are seldom read by dramatists, almost never by actors; therefore, in spite of the testimony of brilliant critics, there has been propagated the false conception that the art of the Meininger rested solely on dazzling costumes and noisy mob scenes.

Before the picture becomes even more indistinct and distorted, it seems to me necessary to unroll it again; and I may well be the one to undertake this, for I belonged to the Meiningen Court Theatre even before its guest tours made it famous. I was privileged to participate in the first guest tour and was active in the last. What I did not learn from my own observation, I was able to learn from the Duke and his wife, for I had the good fortune to become the director at Meiningen on the stage where I had taken my first clumsy steps. I therefore believe that I am duly qualified to write the story of the Meininger.

Max Grube

Meiningen

2 Hans Herrig, *Die Meininger und Ihre Gastspiele.* Dresden, 1897.
3 Robert Prölss, *Das Herzoglich Meiningen'sche Hoftheater und die Bühnenreform.* Erfurt, 1882.
4 Karl Grube, *Die Meininger.* Berlin, n.d.
5 Adolf Winds, *Geschichte der Regie.* Berlin, 1925.
6 Karl Frenzel, *Berliner Dramaturgie.* Hannover, 1897.
7 Heinrich Bulthaupt, *Dramaturgie der Klassiker.* Oldenburg, 1893.

CHAPTER I

THE GERMAN STAGE BEFORE THE
APPEARANCE OF THE MEININGER

The most remarkable thing about the first appearance of the Meininger was that they stepped upon the stage a fully experienced company. Their initial attempts, at first timid and then ever more daring, their long years of preparation in the isolation of the beautiful little town on the Werra— these had not been heeded, indeed had hardly been noticed.

Like a surprising meteor they rose in the theatre heaven.

Don Philipp's words, "The surprising succeeds,"[8] are especially valid for the theatre. Although a personality or theatrical piece may slowly and gradually struggle into the favor of the public, this is unusual. The first impression tends to be the decisive one; and in this instance, it was overwhelming. I have witnessed many great theatre successes, but I have never heard a more powerful storm of applause than that which first roared through the Friedrich-Wilhelm-Städtisches-Theater on that First of May, 1874. Those on the stage, who are always more sensitive to applause than is the audience which is producing it, were aware that here were two distinct kinds of approval. First they heard that applause which cannot wait for the fall of the curtain, which breaks forth just as the curtain starts descending: "the desire to praise long held in check," which releases the first enthusiasm of the audience. Then followed that other, thoughtful applause, which begins only after a pause filled with tense emotion.

The critics joined the acclamation of the public. Only a few voices felt it necessary to admonish and censure. These men pronounced the new constellation brilliant, but deceptive. The most notable of these opposing critics was Paul Lindau.[9] Yet it is well known that from this Saul later emerged a Paul who even became Intendant of the Meiningen Court Theatre. The other adverse voices, too, gradually became silent in the storm of praise.

To understand this unheard-of success, one must realize the condition of the German theatre at that time. If one wished to be tactful, he might

---

[8] In Friedrich Schiller's *Don Carlos* (1787), Act III, Sc. 3.
[9] Paul Lindau (1839-1919), novelist, dramatist, and critic, was one of the most distinguished journalists of the day. After the period of the guest tours, he served as Intendant at Meiningen (1895-1899).

• 5

describe it as a "Sleeping Beauty." The German stage had already entered into what may be called its fourth period. As an example of the first period one can point out the *Haupt-und Staatsaktionen*.[10] Then followed a second period, one of development, together with a struggle of theatrical people for artistic recognition and social equality. In the quarrel with arrogant and reactionary men, the free, enlightened geniuses—Lessing and others—emerged as victors. The theatre was now extravagantly praised as advancing moral standards; yet it was also appreciated for its importance as a bearer of culture.

The third period, starting perhaps after the Wars of Independence,[11] is at present highly overrated. The reactionary spirit had paralyzed every free spiritual movement, so that only shooting matches and choral festivals had a universal appeal for general audiences. Literature and art remained the only provinces in which educated Germans could agree with any degree of solidarity.

Since participation in the plastic arts was sharply limited, and since even music, a peculiarly German art, did not influence the wide circles it does today, the theatre became the focal point of all artistic aspirations. The rapturous enthusiasm on the part of young girls and school boys which today glorifies the actor—although usually only in the smaller towns—was in those days his very life's blood. A glance into the literary magazines of that day is sufficient to uncover reviews whose excesses strike us now as almost comical. Only the caustic critic, Saphir,[12] and similar writers of the period acted as a counterbalance. These critics, however, must be regarded not only by their poor victims, but by every unprejudiced reader today as outrageous, scandalous, and even libelous.

A reaction from these excesses had to follow. In the 1840's politics appeared as ruler of the world stage. Through the propaganda drama of Das Junge Deutschland[13] the theatre showed a real progress; yet this was a deceptive bloom, for these dramas were merely means to a goal lying outside of art. Before the 1860's were over, they faded from the stage. The

---

10These were not independent types of drama, as was long thought. The early English comedians played only the violent and melodramatic parts of Marlowe and Shakespeare before their German audiences.When the Germans imitated them, they turned out pieces "full of sound and fury, signifying nothing." These horrific German plays were called *Haupt-und Staatsaktionen,* meaning dramas about "heads-of-state."

11C. 1813.

12Moritz Gottlieb Saphir (1795-1858), literary and theatre critic, had to change his occupation and residence often because of his sharp wit. In 1834 he settled in Vienna and began in 1837 to publish the satiric *Der Humorist.* His sharply malicious wit, so feared by his contemporaries, seems somewhat insipid today.

13The Young Germany Movement was begun in the 1830's by a group of German writers in opposition to the nature poetry and historical dramas of the Romantic period. Openly sympathetic toward the liberals of the Paris Revolution of 1830, they supported a democratic and nationalistic theatre and demanded that it be in opposition to anything reactionary. Their aims and ideas were extensions of those of the Storm and Stress period of half a century earlier. The most notable drama to come from this period is the tragedy celebrating free thought, *Uriel Acosta,* by Karl Gutzkow (1811-1879), a leader of the movement. In it Gutzkow makes a strong plea for tolerance.

classics, too, were exhausted by repeated performances; therefore, the fourth period of our theatre history was a time of debilitation, greatly aggravated by the fact that the theatre had now become merely a commercial undertaking.

With a few laudable exceptions, such as Immermann[14] and Laube,[15] directors in what I have here called the fourth period fastened their eyes on the money bags. One cannot altogether blame them, for cities regarded their theatres not as seats of culture, but rather as sources of revenue to be leased to the highest bidder. Even in Berlin and Vienna there appeared the theatre speculators, Cerf and Carl, for whom any expedient "to fill the money chest" was acceptable. Their last successor was Pollini in Hamburg, who, it must be admitted, stood many degrees higher than they. As a good merchant, he realized that only the best merchandise could fill the stores; the best talent, the theatres. He understood how to assemble the best skills, but the final goal for him, too, was making money.

The court theatres were conducted on a high level, but were often influenced by the caprice and personal preferences of the ruling prince. These court stages could not halt the general decline in the theatre; for, in the face of the new radical playwriting, they had to exercise the most careful restraint, even to the point of rejecting new plays. Freytag's *The Journalists,*[16] for example, was not accepted for production at the Royal Playhouse in Berlin. Certainly some credit must be given to the court theatres, for there the art of the actor was fostered for its own sake. Indeed, it was so nourished that, growing more and more insolent, the actor—who should be merely the servant of the poet's words—became the master. The management was not strong enough to hold a tight rein on the actor, a situation that will be discussed in more detail later. Only under Immermann, Laube, Devrient,[17] Dingelstedt,[18] and later under Putlitz[19] and Wolzogen[20] was the management strictly and methodically operated. They complete the list of Intendants who pursued truly artistic goals; and even these men wasted their powers in struggles and dissentions with superior authority, but mainly with their own performers.

The star system, which had spread its roots in the previous period, suddenly bloomed in this fourth period of German theatre history. The public, having become theatre weary, patronized classical pieces only when some noted guest artist assumed a leading role. The names of Sydelmann,

14Karl Immermann (1796-1840) contributed greatly to the experimental theatre during his three year management in Düsseldorf (1838-1840).
15Heinrich Laube (1806-1884) served as director of the Vienna Burgtheater (1849-1866). He improved the acting of the company, raised the standards of training, and enlarged the repertory of the theatre.
16A realistic comedy of newspaper life written in 1853 by Gustav Freytag. It is his best known play.
17Philipp Eduard Devrient (1801-1877), director of the Court Theatre, Dresden (1844-46), Karlsruhe Theatre (1852-70).
18Franz von Dingelstedt (1814-1881), poet and dramatist. Intendant of the Court Theatres at Munich (1850-56), Weimar (1857-67), and Vienna (1872-80).
19Gustav von Putlitz (1821-1890), novelist and dramatist.
20Ernst, Baron von Wolzogen (1855-1934), dramatist, novelist, and Director of the Vienna Court Theatre.

Wilhelm Kunst, Emil Devrient, Bogumil Davison, and Friedrich Haase[21] are still well remembered. But it is probably less well known that a whole multitude of stars proved their powers of attraction on the smaller stages. When, at the beginning of the 1870's, I made a tour through the Erz Mountains in Saxony with a traveling troupe, I learned that even those audiences whom we looked down upon as "guinea pigs" possessed their favorite. His name was Leichsenring. Unfortunately, I never saw him. He demanded a salary of five *taler;* and since the manager of our company could not comply with such demands, the negotiations had to be broken off.

Clearly, resident actors working under such circumstances had to regard themselves as gods of the lesser tribes. The guest stars not only pocketed larger sums, but as much as possible they demanded that the effective scenes of all other roles be deleted. With inadequate rehearsals, at which only the scenes of the guest artist were carefully rehearsed, the performances of the others were greatly weakened. How could an actor find genuine happiness in such work? Indifference, careless rehearsing, and imperfect learning gained ground, and ultimately began to reveal themselves in a slovenliness which today would not be tolerated in even the smallest theatre.

Let no one believe that I exaggerate here. I myself have had such experiences. Theatre anecdotes furnish striking proof of my statements— anecdotes which in those days rose like mushrooms from the stage floor, and which today, even outside the theatre, are still repeated. The point of the joke always rested on the defects of the scenery, the properties, or the costumes, and on slips of memory and that sort of thing. Anyone who was active on the stage at that time must certainly recognize in these little stories a mirror accurately reflecting theatrical conditions then. The present day stage no longer furnishes such anecdotes. Since the Meininger set in motion the faltering clockwork of the stage, the movement is more exact than at any time before.

The result of the Meininger reforms—although there were naturally the exceptions that proved the rule—was a genuine uniformity of style in the performance of tragedy; I must say, however, that in later years only the Burgtheater has consistently done justice to the very high artistic standards of the Meininger.

In any case, the declamatory Weimar manner had little by little become

---

[21]Germany's greatest actors of the early and middle nineteenth century: Karl Seydelmann (1795-1843), a realistic actor as well as the author of several dramas; Wilhelm Kunst (1799-1859), outstanding in the role of Karl Moor in Schiller's *The Robbers,* and in the roles of Othello and of Graf von Strahl in von Kleist's *Kathy from Heilbronn;* Gustav Emil Devrient (1803-1872), the youngest and most gifted of the famous acting family, which besides his brothers, Karl August (1797-1872), and Philipp Eduard (1801-1877), included his uncle Ludwig (1784-1832), and his nephew, Otto (1838-1894). All were famous as managers, playwrights, and actors, especially in the plays of Shakespeare and Schiller. Gustav Emil gained outstanding fame in the plays of Shakespeare and in Schiller's *Don Carlos.* When he played Hamlet in London, his performance was said to equal that of Edmund Kean; Bogumil Davison or Dawison (1818-1872), born in Warsaw, became one of the greatest German Shakespearean actors of his time; Friedrich Haase (1827-1911) played in all the leading theatres of Germany and made successful appearances in Russia and the United States. He managed the Court Theatre in Coburg and the Municipal Theatre in Leipzig before moving to Berlin, where he founded and managed the Deutsches Theater.

universally accepted; but now, stimulated by the example of Seydelmann and especially of Davison, actors began to cultivate a more natural diction. The difference in the two styles of acting was immediately noticeable on the court stages, yet both continued to be seen. The established artists on such stages could not be summarily removed to make way for younger actors dedicated to the new style—or one might better say, to the renaissance of an old one. For the native German manner of acting in which Iffland,[22] Schröder,[23] and Fleck[24] had been brilliant was just the opposite of the French declamatory manner, the ruling style in the time of Gottsched[25] and later revived by Goethe.[26]

The audience, however, did not place great worth on this striving for a uniform style; the theatre-goer had been accustomed to regard the performance of the actor as the special object of his consideration. Let each actor show his own particular style to best advantage! Emil Devrient, the most finished representative of the Weimar school, and Davison, the brilliant realist burdened by no tradition, were equally applauded.

On many stages the ensemble was praised, but it was not ensemble playing as we know it today, in which even the smallest part, well-cast, performs its own special action (yet I must mention that often these minor actors push themselves forward annoyingly). Then ensemble playing consisted more of the adaptation of skills through long acting together. Frequently it was only an art in which one actor covered up the mistakes of another. The catchword of the theatre was "routine,"[27] a word one does not find in the vocabulary of the modern actor. Of course, there are actors who depend entirely on routine, but nothing genuine will come from them.

The French influence prevailed in all matters of stage machinery and decor. Famous among others were the stage settings in Darmstadt, where Karl Brandt, the founder of a whole generation of theatre technicians (as one called them in those days—now they carry the title of Technical Director), produced wonderful technical effects, but these were only for the benefit of the opera.

The theatre had to content itself with the cast-off scenery of the opera; it was dependent on a general stock, the so-called *fundus instructus*. This contained a number of settings which appeared in every play. There were the "wild" and the "open" forest scene, the "free tract of country," the

---

22August Wilhelm Iffland (1759-1814), a virtuoso actor-dramatist, went to Weimar as a leading actor under Goethe, but soon left for Berlin, where he headed the Royal Playhouse until 1814. *The Huntsmen*, a somewhat realistic play, is his most famous.
23Friedrich Ludwig Schröder (1744-1816), actor, manager, dramatist, is generally considered the best German tragic actor of his century. He was a fine ensemble player and established high standards of acting and directing.
24Friedrich Ferdinand Fleck (1757-1801) was a gifted but uneven actor who created the role of Wallenstein.
25Johann Christoph Gottsched (1700-1766), poet and critic, made a valiant effort to reform the German stage by creating his own company and opening his own theatre with the great actress, Karolina Neuber, as the leading artist. He was influenced by French neo-classicism and translated Corneille's *Le Cid* and Racine's *Iphigénie* into German. Lessing later attacked his ideas ruthlessly.
26Johann Wolfgang von Goethe (1749-1832) is so famous as Germany's greatest poet that it is easy to forget that for many years he was Intendant at the Weimar Court Theatre (1791-1817).
27Grube uses this same word.

Park, the "old German" and the "modern" city, the "hall of the knights," etc. It never occurred to the director to have a set designed for a play or to make sure that a poetic work should have its own characteristic scenery. The style of the costumes, which for the most part was very poor, we shall discuss at a more suitable time.

Such conditions were not likely to promote a desire for the drama. "The cultured people had been acted out of the theatre," was the opinion of Eduard Devrient in his history of the German theatre,[28] still an admirable one although there have been later theatre histories published.

Into this stifling atmosphere the Meininger flashed as a purifying bolt of lightning!

On the evening of May 1, 1874, the weather was fine. Although fine weather is always harmful to the theatre, the Friedrich-Wilhelm-Städtisches (now the Deutsches) Theater was sold out. What one might call "all Berlin" was there. One really had to be present! There was going to be something quite new: an entire group of actors in a guest appearance! An ensemble with all scenery, properties, costumes, and weapons! Everyone had read about it in the newspapers. Everyone waited for the wonderful things that were to come, waited with that superior smile peculiar to the inhabitants of the young capital city. Wilhelm von Humboldt criticized them somewhat unkindly, when, in a letter, he said, "The Berliners sit in their boxes like executioners."

Scenery! Costumes! As if everyone in Berlin had not seen the most wonderful examples of these arts! The performance was the important thing. Did this little court theatre of an infinitesimal principality intend to show the Royal Theater how to act? Would these unknown players enter into competition with Döring, Berndel, Maxim Ludwig, with Ehrhart, Klara Meyer, or Frieb-Blumauer?[29] After all, Meiningen! What good could come from Nazareth?

But it did come, and it took the critical Berliners by storm. For the curtain rose on a little court theatre, but it descended on a famous troupe. The "Meininger" was established.

---

[28]Eduard Devrient, *Geschichte der deutschen Schauspielkunst.* Berlin, 1905.
[29]The reputation of none of these actors, so notable in the late nineteenth century, has survived.

CHAPTER II

THE EARLY HISTORY OF THE MEININGEN COURT THEATRE

Who up to that time had ever spoken of Meiningen? Who would even have been aware of it, had there not been in the little Duchy a fashionable health resort, Liebenstein, much visited by Berliners? There visitors had seen the tall figure of the reigning Duke mingling now and then with the guests of the resort, or even had seen His Serene Highness taking coffee under the linden trees of the resort garden. The Duke, so it was said, was believed to be a special patron of the Court Theatre. This, however, was very common in the small capitals.

On the other hand, a great sensation had been stirred up by the fact that in March of the previous year the Duke had elevated the principal actress of his troupe, a Miss Ellen Franz, to be his wife. To be sure, princes and theatre-princesses had been drawn together before into sentimental bonds; indeed, a few princely persons had so far forgotten their position as to form misalliances, but a reigning Prince, a Duke by the Grace of God—even if it was only of a small country—and an actress! That was unheard of! Yet, in the last analysis, it was in a very small state, and the incident was not world shattering; soon everyone returned to the usual order of affairs. Perhaps during the summer of 1873 Bad Liebenstein saw a few more curious guests than usual, but the short journey to the Residenz attracted none of them.

Even in literary circles it was probably unknown that theatre history—certainly not epoch-making, yet not entirely uninteresting—had been made here in Meiningen in the course of the previous century. Research into theatre history as it is now springing up through the efforts of Litzmann, Hermann, Wolff, and other scholars was then unknown.

As early as the eighteenth century, long before she had possession of a theatre building, Thalia was a welcome guest in the charmingly situated little town on the Werra. Like many larger places the town knew the art of the theatre—which was still controversial and still under attack—only through traveling troupes. Of course, all educated circles were disposed to be friendly to it; and even where the theatre could find no permanent abode, it was lovingly cultivated by those who cherished it.

In Meiningen the court circles of the late eighteenth century devoted themselves to this agreeable undertaking with the greatest fervor, and the enthusiasts took their duties very seriously. One of the principal actors was the ruling Prince;[30] his younger brother also performed with enthusiasm.[31] These noble dilettantes set for themselves high goals. Among the plays presented were Leisewitz's *Julius of Tarento,* Wieland's *Jane Grey,* Diderot's *The Father of the Family,* and Voltaire's *The Coffee House,* as well as the old Essex drama, *The Favor of the Prince,* which, as is well known, was composed by four poets.

Amateur comedy was also played at Gotha and at many other small courts; but the Meiningen company is distinguished by the publication of a special edition containing many of the works it presented. As curiosities the Ducal Library preserves perhaps the only copies of *The Favor of the Prince,* given in May 1776; *The Father of the Family,* August 12, 1776; *The Mailcoach* by Ayrenhoff, November 1776; *The Scotchwoman* or *The Coffee House,* August 10, 1778; and *Julius of Tarento,* 1780.[32] On some of these pieces is the note: To be found in the court printing presses.

These books came into the world sometimes in the best form, but more often in the worst. Yet they give evidence of the literary tendencies of the royal theatre enthusiast, Prince Karl August, whose name unfortunately has not come down through history as has that of his namesake in Weimar.[33] Nevertheless, he was no undistinguished man. In his travel letters he proves himself a good observer by his judgment of such men as Lavater, Basedow, Bodmer, and Gessner. About Goethe, with whom he became acquainted in Frankfurt, he wrote on February 4, 1775:

> Herr Goethe ate with us at midday. I was pleased that he sat beside me, so that I could observe him more closely. He talks a great deal and very well. He is extremely artless and is astonishingly amusing and jolly. He is tall and well built, like Gotter in stature.[34] He has his own particular manners, for he really belongs to a particular race of men. He has his own ideas and opinions about all things; about the men he knows, he has his own individual language, his own words.

And on the 23rd of May:

> This afternoon as I sat in my room and read with Herr Heim in Chronegk's *The First Bloom of the Spirit,* a servant came in and said that a Doctor from Frankfurt wished to speak to me; I was

30The ruling Duke, Karl August, came to the throne in 1765. He died in 1782 and was succeeded by his brother, Georg I.

31Georg I, who occupied the ducal throne from 1782-1806, was intensely interested in all things literary and theatrical. He was acquainted with Goethe and was instrumental in obtaining a position at Jena for Schiller. Grube discusses in some detail the innovations Georg I instituted in the Meiningen theatre and points out that his grandson, Georg II, Director of the Meininger, had ample family precedent for his interests.

32All these copies have since been lost.

33The name of Duke Karl August (1757-1828) has a place in history because it was during his rule that Goethe made Weimar a center of literature, science, art, and liberal political thought. Goethe attracted such men as Herder and Schiller, improved the physical appearance of the city, and managed the state theatre, presenting many of his and Schiller's plays for the first time.

34Friedrich Wilhelm Gotter (1746-1797), poet and playwright, director of the Gotha Theatre. His *Geisterinsel,* adapted from Shakespeare's *Tempest,* was praised by Goethe.

not surprised when Doctor Goethe entered. Yes, it was he himself; he had come from Frankfurt to visit his sister in Baden. In Karlsruhe he had spoken to the Royal Family of Weimar and was here to see his friend Lenz. He insisted that he sit beside me on the sofa. I like Goethe; he is so natural.

Unfortunately, this art-loving young prince, Karl August, died in his twenty-eighth year. His younger brother, Georg I, who had come of age on February 4, 1782, and who had been made co-regent with him, succeeded him. At the same time the new Duke took over the guidance of the theatre, although by 1781 it drew support less from court circles than from middle-class society. Yet the court had not entirely withdrawn from the theatre, and now as before the reigning Duke took an active part as an actor.

This noble friend of art, who afterwards granted refuge to Jean Paul[35] for two years, should also be thanked for summoning Schiller to Jena and later appointing him as Court Councillor. Schiller's request for this appointment, which he wished to offer to his bride as the equivalent of a noble title, is still preserved. It is true that later Schiller designated himself as Court Councillor of the Saxe-Weimar Court; probably the title was bestowed reciprocally by both courts as a designation of merit from Meiningen, Coburg-Gotha, and Altenburg.

The young sovereign seems to have busied himself with the direction of the theatre and considered the playing of comedy as a really serious business. If his grandson, Georg II, ultimately turned his attention wholeheartedly to the theatre, one might say it is pure evidence of artistic atavism.

Meiningen saw its first professional company when Schönemann[36] appeared there in 1785. In 1787 performances were given for the court by Sondershausen; in 1790, by a director, Weber; and in 1795, by Hasslock.

The city acquired its first theatre building in 1831.[37] The money was raised through a successful sale of stock which showed the enthusiasm of the citizens in a gratifying manner. There were shares at 50 *gulden* with a choice of 3% or 4% interest or bearing no interest at all. Eighty-seven citizens of Meiningen selected shares at 3% interest, eighty-five took shares at 4% interest, and 252 took shares without demanding any interest.

On December 17, the birthday of Duke Bernhard Erich Freund,[38] the theatre opened with *Fra Diavalo*. Beckstein gave a suitable prologue. The theatre was leased to companies who were active in the vicinity: Erfurt, Bamberg, etc. The Duke granted an allowance of 250 *gulden* monthly, and

---

35 Johann Paul Richter, pseud. Jean Paul (1763-1825), German romantic novelist and dramatist.
36 Johann Friedrich Schönemann (b. 1704). Not an inspired actor, but a talented leader, he helped raise the standards of the German theatre and attracted gifted actors to his company.
37 Before 1831, performances were given in a large ballroom on the third floor of the castle.
38 Bernhard Erich Freund (1800-1882), son of Georg I, became the ruling Duke upon the death of his father in 1806. During his minority, he ruled through a Regent.

after the expenses of a performance had been met, the earnings amounted to about 1000 *gulden*. It was not unusual for the Duke to increase his subsidy to attract some artist that appealed to him. The few records still extant consist for the most part of letters from the directors begging for greater support. In these instances, the Duke shows himself almost always generous, even to the entreaties of individual members of the troupe.

Literary excellence was not demanded of these companies. A little discovery that I made when I was thinning out old scenery is perhaps typical. I uncovered among other things the pasteboard "marble" horse from which the Commander on a Horse[39] may have bowed down to the crowd. The construction is not bad. Only the inscription on the base calls forth misgivings: in foot high letters there stands:

Die Rache erwartet hier dem Mörder.[40]

Thus vengeance had waited year after year without any spectators taking offense at its not completely faultless German. As an apology for the public, it can be said that the moonlight in the Meiningen Cemetery of Seville was so weak that no one could read this important inscription. But certainly it should have been shocking to the director.

Perhaps it had been prepared during the inglorious tenure of Count Hahn, who wore the gold paper crown in the year 1836. This theatre count did not "stand on the best terms with *mir* and *mich*,"[41] as his repeated petitions to His Highness reveal. His luck in Meiningen was not propitious, a fact for which he himself was mostly to blame. On November 10, 1836, the Royal Theatre Commission reproaches him: he needs a good first tenor, a first bass, a first comic bass, and a prima donna. Furthermore, any future performance of the opera is forbidden until the personnel has reached a standard previously agreed upon, and the extra subsidy is to be stopped. Soon, it appears that the subsidy was renewed on the entreaty of the Count.

By the year 1837 the aristocratic theatre enthusiast, Hahn—who, as Karl von Holtei told me, had displayed his dramatic skills in thunder and lightning and in painting the supernumeraries[42]—had disappeared from the scene. Most of the directors who followed him had no better success. Among these may be mentioned the well-known theatre agent, Ferdinand Roeder. Only one of the directors, Bömly, remained a second winter.

Finally, in 1860, wearied by these conditions, Duke Bernhard changed the subsidized theatre into a real one. As in Berlin a young officer, Botho von Hülsen, had been made Intendant, so here too a Lieutenant, Baron von Stein, was assigned to this duty. Unlike his colleague in Berlin, von Stein struggled vigorously against the honor, but in vain. He proved to be extremely valuable, though, especially as he had the good fortune of having

---

39The Commendatore, *Don Giovanni*, Act II, Sc. 3.

40Grube is pointing out that neither the director nor the audience noticed the error in grammar, the dative case for the accusative: "Vengeance here awaits the murderer."

41*i.e.*, his grammar was often incorrect.

42The practice of painting the mobs and extras on the backdrop instead of having real people on the stage persisted in some German theatres as late as 1900.

in Dr. Locher a first-rate director. The repertoire, which up to that time had seldom included classical works, improved gratifyingly.

Earlier, in the year 1844, a masterpiece, *Antigone,* was produced on an authentic antique stage. In contrast to most of the productions, it was well attended, as was the comedy, *The Dog of Montardis.*[43] The clever dog, Dragon, wagged his tail across the stage many times, attracting others besides the subscription holders. On the playbill a note was inserted: "At the appearance of the dog, please be as quiet as possible."

Another program note furnishes a little companion piece to the inscription on the base of the Commander's horse:

Raphael and his ideal Madonna, appearing to him as a vision; a living picture artistically executed by the court painter, Herr Schellhorn, and accompanied by tender sounding harmony.

In 1839 Kunst entertained as guest star eight times with the greatest success. After he had already given his farewell performance, he had to perform on the ninth evening as Aballino, the great bandit. His repertoire was varied enough: *Hamlet;* the head forester in Iffland's *The Huntsmen;* the king in *Pigtail and Sword; Tell; Wallenstein; Lear;* and in between, *Hinko the Freedman,* the drawing card of Birch-Pfeiffer, and a long forgotten comedy by Theodor Apel, *The Young Seamstress.*

In 1857 an artistic production of *A Midsummer Night's Dream* was given as a festival offering on the birthday of Crown Prince Georg. It is likely that Georg had expressed a definite wish in this case, for his interest in the drama was deepening. Ira Aldridge,[44] who appeared at the court in 1857, dedicated to him a little notebook with the translation of the role of Macbeth. Besides Othello, the Black Beast (as von Holtei was accustomed to call the remarkable Negro) played Macbeth and Shylock. With *The Merchant of Venice* he presented the one-act blackface farce, *The Padlock.* In it the leading role of Mungo Park had been especially written for him,[45] and in this performance he did complete justice to the name von Holtei had given him. After *Macbeth* the theatre bill announced *The Farewell,* written in German and spoken by Ira Aldridge.

Young Prince Georg's interest and activity in the theatre had increased after his father, whose politics leaned toward those of Austria, brought him back from Berlin. The Prince, then a Major of the First Guard Regiment, had returned much against his will. It was his heartfelt wish, as I have heard from his own lips, to pursue a military career. Kind destiny ordained it otherwise, and instead of a commander of armies Germany gained a commander of art.

Later the Duke's royal conduct displayed his soldierly propensities: he staged war and battle scenes with special enthusiasm. "During a battle, all run about," he was accustomed to say. Accordingly, as an example,

---

[43]This trivial farce by Guilbert de Pixérécourt was along with his other fairy tales, melodramas, and costume pieces extraordinarily successful.
[44]Ira Aldridge (1810-1866), American Negro actor.
[45]Does Grube mean that the role was especially adapted for Aldridge? *The Padlock* by Isaac Bickerstaffe was first performed at Drury Lane in 1768.

Illo, Terzky, and Neumann, the Captain of the Cavalry, in the third act of *Wallenstein's Death,* had to enter and exit in a great hurry—almost on the run. This commotion with the threatening insurrection in the camp imparted a unique character to the act, an excitement which communicated itself to the audience. It is certainly to be doubted, of course, whether in a modern battle directed from a distance by telephone and telegraph, such commotion prevails.

With what penetrating attention Prince Georg set about guiding the theatre is apparent from a letter which he directed to Intendant von Stein in January 1864. A second letter, in the same vein and addressed to Intendant Bodenstedt, was written after he had become Duke Georg II.

i

January 1864.

Concerning the opera, *Margarete* [*Faust*], allow me to make some observations which I wish you to refer to the stage manager.

1. The appearance of Margarete in the first act: her left arm rests on a little table with slender legs. From a distance, the arm seems to be floating on air. It would be better if this little table were covered with the dark blue cloth which I presented to the property room. If this is done, the effect would be more attractive.

2. Crowd scene: It is a pity that at the performance the business of placing the actors on the tables as the director ordered in rehearsal was omitted. In that manner the group on the left, especially, would attract the attention of the audience.

3. The first entrance of Margarete: She would appear more maidenly, if she did not remain standing near Faust, but crossed the stage without delay. Her solo is so short that this is practical. Faust must walk backwards before her, then move away from her up to the wings.

4. Scene with the jewel casket: a more beautiful case, and within it a mirror to be taken out. In place of a gentleman's golden chain, a lady's necklace—such a one is in the property room.

5. Moonlight: this must begin the very moment that Mephisto orders Nature "to breathe voluptuousness"—in Berlin, if I remember correctly, a magical moonlight spell suffused the landscape. If there are some blue silk lampshades available, these could be drawn in front of the lamps to produce a blue luster which must also be visible in the background.

I believe that the garden scene would be more effective if Margarete's house were standing back behind the next border and the light of the moon came from the other side. Then it would not only strike the walls of the house, but, more importantly, the countenance of Margarete would not be constantly in the shadow, as is now the case.

6. The arrangement of the war scene is certainly a horror—at least, to my taste. The much discussed goose-step is quite out of place here. I think it would be more effective to alter the whole scene. As it is now, one gets the idea that the medieval soldiers who sing in the Soldiers' Chorus are soldiers according to our present-day standards. Let sixteen soldiers be put in brown uniforms (Wallenstein) and the singers in medieval battle apparel of different kinds, using coats of armor and both open-faced and spiked helmets. Three tall under officers should be in sets of armor from the property room. One might look like Dr. Locher when he played Götz.[46]

At the beginning of the scene before the soldiers appear, women and children should be seen running across the stage, in and out, expressing joyful expectation. Then the soldiers appear, singing; the women and children run ahead of them, gathering and grouping on both sides of the stage. The singing warriors march in quickly to martial tempo, but not in rank and file; instead, they enter in a crowd with joyful gestures—by this, I mean swinging weapons, and here and there, hats. The soldiers, to whom the three knights attach themselves, move to the right side of the stage and stand so closely together that the audience can see past them to the left. After this crowd has arranged itself, the sixteen soldiers march in. The leader himself stops near the wings and commands: "Halt!" "Front!" (softly) when the last row of the company has entered.

This group, in two ranks, must march in so that the left group stands somewhat to the rear of those at the right. (See drawing.) After the soldiers, who enter with their lances up, stand at ease, they bring their lances "to foot." In this way, they move so that they open up ranks a little.

By this means the scene would become an excellent one. That it is possible to do this can hardly be doubted—all the more so, since now there is only a chorus rehearsal. The warrior chorus could be provided with battle-axes, maces, and the like. Weapons, such as the two-handed sword, can be obtained from the Henneberger collection—shields and spears, too. The stage manager should direct the entrances from behind the scene. It would be best if he were costumed as a knight à la Götz. If the soldiers stood in the hallway in front of the property room before the scene began, they could march on stage with a "right face," while the Soldier Chorus marched on with a "left face."

7. Mephisto ought not be compelled to stand beside the organ in order to sing; he should be able to project the song even if the

[46]Hero of Goethe's *Götz von Berlichingen* (1773).

organ is on the opposite side of the stage. Then the praying people, instead of kneeling with their faces to the side altar where Margarete is kneeling, could be turned in the opposite direction and always see the choir master merely by turning their heads. They should enter from the opposite side and kneel, if possible, farther in the background. In this scene the stage is lighted too brightly. There is enough light if the audience can see the features of Margarete clearly. If the stage is dim, all the better. If the praying congregation is arranged as I suggest, the members would not observe the shocking expression of Gretchen and not be aware when she falls into a faint. She would then lie there unnoticed by the congregation; this would make a stronger impression on the audience.

8. The prison scene: A flat mattress covered with straw would be better than the present wooden-plank bed. The mattress can be dragged off, leaving the straw lying there, so that it will not disturb the last scene, the apotheosis. With our present means, this last scene is not successful.

9. The apotheosis: The group in the background may be too symmetrical. The audience cannot see the angels' wings, for they are too white. If they were painted in dark rainbow colors, they would stand out from the background.

i i

February 1867.

Can you not arrange a special correspondence in the local daily newspaper about the *Caesar* performance and in the article explain what the three new sets really represent? The Weimar scene painter still had the Visconti sketch.[47] I'll have to send for it, because in it are named the various buildings of the Roman Forum. The local public must be prepared for the next performance of *Caesar*.

First set: The Capitol as seen from the Forum. The substructure of the middle building still stands today, as does the tower. Above to the right there stands the temple of Zeus Capitolinis. The Via Sacra leads under the outside staircase to an arch on the left and down to the left side of the Capitoline middle building. Second set: Legislative Assembly of Pompey, where the Senate sat in conference in the year of Caesar's death because the Senators' Assembly Hall in the Forum had been burned during the Civil Wars. In the foreground is an open space with the Curia opening into it. The assemblies of the Senate take place outside before the people. The throne of Caesar stands between the

---

[47]Ennio Quirino Visconti (1751-1818), Italian archeologist and conservator of the Capitoline Museum, Rome. A political refugee in Paris after 1799, he became curator of antiquities at the Louvre. He wrote the first volume of *Iconographie romaine* (1817).

curial benches in front of which is the recently restored statue of Pompey. This statue is a copy of the one in Rome, which was excavated in the Curia of Pompey and is therefore the one that stood in the Curia. The original is marble, three feet high. (At this point there were some remarks about the clever use of space between the columns.)[48] An addition to Shakespeare's text: "Cursed Caesar, what are you doing?" and "Brothers, help!" according to Plutarch. Caesar grasps Casca by the arm and wounds him with a stylus. (Caesar's costume according to the Roman authors.) (Masks of Caesar and Brutus from coins.) Third setting for the Roman Forum (the designation of the buildings according to the Visconti drawings). [Plate IV A] Place the Rostrum with the front facing the Curia, the narrow side to the crowd. (The byplay of the crowd is produced through the actors and the extras.) Fourth and fifth acts: The javelins, weapons invented for use against Pyrrhus, with which the Romans won their victories, just as the Prussians with their needle-guns, etc., etc. . . .

The most experienced stage manager could not have expressed more pertinent remarks. Certainly the writer had found opportunity to study the theatre in Berlin and Munich, Paris and London—and had made good use of it. From the letter to von Stein, it is evident that the Crown Prince found only a modest collection of costumes. Where and when he could, he lent the assistance of his restricted purse. Albert Ellmenreich, the father of Franziska, has said that at times in Meiningen all forms of garniture—by garniture in the theatre he meant costumes and properties—were missing. On the other hand, the armory contained hundreds of daggers which the Crown Prince had given to it. The old actor probably had not counted the hundred daggers himself, but very likely he was right.

The year 1866 brought to Duke Bernhard Erich Freund the fruits of his misplaced political allegiance, and he was forced to abdicate in favor of his son. As Georg II, the new Duke became not only the constitutional monarch of his country, but also the undisputed head of the Court Theatre.

48Grube's parentheses.

CHAPTER III

GEORG II

Is it difficult not to write a panegyric.[49]

But why should I impose restrictions upon myself? Why should I not conform to the truth in saying that this Prince, this extraordinary man and artist, is deserving and worthy of every song of praise? Not only as a conscientious historian should I endeavor to emphasize his positive qualities, but I am forced to do so by a love of truth.

Year after year, I lived in the company of this unusual man. In the last years of his life I had the good fortune to enjoy his confidential association for all too short a time, since he resided in Meiningen only a few weeks in winter. I could never uncover any dark sides to his nature, and I was always under the spell of his pure and honorably aristocratic personality.

His manners were not condescending, but rather were those of a gentleman. One might think that this would be a matter of course in the so-called highest circles, but I have known many princely persons who thought they were entitled to demand many special privileges. The Duke possessed that courtly manner of heart about which Goethe speaks. As an example, whenever I was invited to Meiningen as a guest star or to attend the performance of some play, the old Grandseigneur always met me at the door of the castle to lead me to my room himself.

His aversion to granting cash advances to the actors — he concerned himself in all matters of the theatre, even the smallest — was almost unconquerable. The money involved was not the point of the question. "My court officers must exist without advances," he was accustomed to say. "Why shouldn't my actors do the same?" And, little by little, they learned to do just that.

He was by no means interested only in the theatre and he never neglected his royal duties for his artistic interests; still he avoided as much as possible the formalities of these duties. Above all else, he was interested in his country and sought to provide himself with the greatest knowledge of it. Once a week he held an audience to which anyone could come without an appointment. Only as his deafness increased did he abandon this fine custom, which his subjects never misused.

His modesty was beyond all praise; never did I hear him mention his

---

[49]"Difficile est panegyricum non scribere."

activities in a self-satisfied or boastful way. He was a thoroughly ingenuous artist; he considered what he had created nothing unusual. To him it was entirely proper that his name should remain in the background, or that the name "The Meininger" had been coined. For a long time people regarded Chronegk as the creator of the Meiningen productions. At no time did the Duke ever allow this to be contradicted. I believe that I was the first to lay the true facts before the general public. When I asked the old Duke once what especially had moved him to take his productions throughout the world on guest appearances, he answered literally, "I was annoyed that Shakespeare was so badly played in Germany."

That this artist-Prince did not devote his entire attention to the theatre has been related elsewhere. His desire for knowledge was as multilateral as his education. Once I had to wait for him quite a while—something that rarely happened — and I noticed on the window casement a choice edition on Japan. I looked into it and was astonished to find several rough sketches on which had been written in the Duke's own hand the names of all the Japanese Emperors, selected from this book.

He had had the good fortune to enjoy a superior education. A clever tutor—we might say one almost as wise as he was affectionate—had carefully watched over the prince entrusted to him. Any person fortunate enough to have access to the letters Moritz Seebeck—later the Privy Councillor and Curator at the University of Jena—addressed to his wife, can glance into a pure and noble soul. Unfortunately, these letters have not yet been made public. Very detailed and beautifully "penned" according to the fashion of the period, they were not intended for publication, for they contain many personal touches and intimate sentiments. They are the unbiased testimony of the finest relations between student and teacher. All the inclination toward nobility and high-mindedness which lay dormant in the talented boy was cleverly and lovingly awakened and encouraged to bloom. Nor did that marked talent for drawing, which early manifested itself, go unnoticed.

Many years later the mature Duke created a second instance of great good fortune for himself, when he had the courage to enter into a marriage of love. Death had already robbed him of two well-born consorts, three Princes secured the succession, and now he dared let his heart speak freely. He wasted little anxiety on the consequences that usually result from a marriage between persons of different rank. His choice reflected honor upon him. Seldom has a union better earned the name of a model marriage than that of Duke Georg of Saxe-Meiningen and the actress, Ellen Franz, to whom he gave the title Baroness von Heldburg.

The Duke took pleasure in all aspects of staging from artistic vision to practical tasks, but the dramatic-literary importance of the Meiningen productions must be ascribed to the influence which the Baroness von Heldburg exercised on her husband.

The Duke's unusual artistic talent was for drawing rather than for painting. "Whenever I have expressed myself in color," he said himself, "people have always found the results terrible." When Kaulbach said to him, "It is too bad that you are a little Prince, you could have become a great painter," he referred to the princely artist's talent for composition, which displayed itself in many sketches and cartoons, greatly influenced by the style of Kaulbach and Cornelius.[50]

All, or at least almost all, the sketches for the stage settings executed at Coburg by that talented theatre painter, Brückner, were designed either by the Duke or were carried out according to his strictest instructions. In addition, the most important groupings in the plays were frequently determined in advance in sketches. The Duke insisted that groups never freeze into living pictures, and these sketches show clearly how the movement was to be realized and presented.

The Duke's vigorous striving for movement is evident in his seascapes, where his efforts were most successful. He belongs to that very small number of artists who paint not only the water and the waves, but also reveal the sea's foaming and roaring. It seems to me that the Duke's seascapes and landscapes are far more outstanding than his figure compositions. [Plate IV B] In the latter he was always somewhat under the influence of a conscious "school" manner. As a landscape artist he achieved an individual style and learned directly from that great schoolmistress, Nature; although, of course, he was no naturalist. His teacher, Seebeck, has handed down a charming remark of the boy. "When I draw figures, I draw them as they should be, but landscapes as they are."

It is well known that the Duke established on his stage a strict insistence upon historically correct costuming, an innovation which has been influential up to the most recent times, when the theatre has turned again to imaginative costumes. The costume sketches at Meiningen were based upon the most exhaustive study. Sketched on large octavo sheets, they are done only in outline, but all the individual characteristics are distinctly apparent. Occasionally, details are noted in the margin. On the evening of a performance, each actor found such a sheet at his place, so that there would be no misunderstanding between him and the wardrobe master about how each piece of costume was to be worn. It was not unusual for the actor to see himself depicted in his role by a few characteristic strokes —almost like a portrait. The designs were executed first in light pencil, later to be erased, then filled in with a quill or an ordinary straight pen and plain ink. These pictures almost always show, too, a distinctive posture of the character.

For the great performances at Vienna, a whole series of drawings were prepared. After one was lost, they were bound together in seven volumes and now remain to give evidence of the ability, the industry, and the

---

[50] Wilhelm von Kaulbach (1805-1874), German historical painter and illustrator, known for his love of the dramatic, his facility for painting on a large scale, and his penchant for the grotesque and satiric. Peter von Cornelius (1783-1867), German fresco painter, also known for his fine illustrations for *Faust* and *The Nibelungenlied*.

knowledge of the princely artist. At first, he saw the theatre as an immense canvas on which he could reveal the most changing, the most beautiful, yet certainly the most transitory pictures. Just as an artist studies a work which he is to illustrate in order to find the potential pictures in it, the Duke at this stage of his development relegated the drama to second place as he created illustrations for "stage poems." That a profound change then occurred—that the plays were later faithfully presented on the stage, that the creator of the Meininger came to recognize fully the essential character of dramatic production, that he became not only an enthusiastic admirer of the classical poets (for he was always that), but that he became an expert classical scholar—for all that, the Duke had to thank his wife from the world of the theatre.

Helene von Heldburg was a life companion who made him deeply happy. This he often told her in his very moving letters, which, even at the most advanced age, he wrote to her whenever they were obliged to be separated. He expressed the same sentiments to me repeatedly. The actress became for him also the cleverest assistant, the wisest and most understanding helper in his life work.

And not only that! This middle-class wife opened up for her princely husband a clear view of all aspects of real life—something the mighty of the world almost always experience only through the medium of court life, which after all presents only a dim reflection of things as they are.

In the history of the theatre, next to the radiant picture of Georg II of Saxe-Meiningen, will shine imperishably that of Helene von Heldburg.

CHAPTER IV

HELENE, BARONESS VON HELDBURG

Ellen Franz, Helene von Heldburg, came from a very good middle-class family, a considerable rarity in the theatre in those days. Her father, Dr. Hermann Franz, was director of a trade school in Berlin; her mother, an English aristocrat, was a Miss Grant. A typical love story: Tutor and Lady! As both parents were cultured and had intellectual interests—Frau Franz had even published a small volume of lyric poems, *Wild Roses*—it was no wonder that their daughter displayed artistic inclinations, which showed themselves first in music. A professional career as a concert artist was her first goal. She began her studies with Kullak, but soon she came to Hans von Bülow[51] with the request that he take her as a pupil.

"With fear and trembling," she related, "I played a little for the Master. When he wished to hear Bach and I told him that Kullak had thought I should attempt Bach later, Bülow spoke these wonderful words: 'Bach is our daily bread.'"

What I was able to produce of Bach must not have appeared insipid to him, for he took me as a pupil. How I honored him! How frightened I was for him at that now famous concert at the singing academy when a Liszt symphony was hissed. Bülow cried out, "Those who are hissing are asked to leave the hall." At these words, very little was needed to change the excitement in the hall to violence.

One day the Master said to me, "Every day you go through my wife's salon. Why don't you visit her?" I had no idea there was a Frau von Bülow, but naturally I took advantage of the hint as soon as possible. Soon the closest friendship bound me to this charming lady.[52] I worshipped this woman, two years older than I, and she called me her little "chicken."

Suddenly the taste for music receded into the background and an affection for the stage emerged. As a concert at which Liszt conducted

[51]Hans Guido von Bülow (1830-1894), pianist and conductor. Upon hearing Liszt conduct *Lohengrin* at Weimar in 1850, Bülow left his legal studies for a musical career, studied under Liszt, and conducted the premieres of several Wagner operas. He became Brahms' most ardent champion. The first of the modern virtuoso conductors, he achieved great distinction as a conductor (1880-1885) of the ducal orchestra at Meiningen. Grube later discusses his break with the Duke.
[52]This is the famous Frau Cosima (1837-1930), the natural daughter of Liszt and the Comtesse d'Agoult. From 1857-1869 she was the wife of von Bülow. In 1870 she married Richard Wagner and identified herself so closely with his work that after his death she became largely responsible for the fame of the Bayreuth festivals.

some of his own works, Fräulein Franz appeared publicly for the first time and successfully delivered Schumann's "Schön Hedwig" and "Heide-knaben."[53]

Her parents vigorously opposed the wishes of their daughter for a theatrical career, and it was only the intervention of Frau Cosima which caused the anxious parents to yield.

After the novice had been instructed for a time by the admirable Frieb-Blumauer, she found her first engagement in the Court Theatre at Saxe-Coburg. This was arranged by no less a person than Franz Liszt, who had met the beginner in Bülow's house. "Albion," as he called her, became his pet. In recommending her, he performed a service not only for her, but also for the Court Theatre, which at that moment was in a serious dilemma. Emil Devrient was to make a guest appearance in eight days as Rochester, and still there was no Jane Eyre.

This role, the most effective that has ever been written,[54] brought to the young novice on September 10, 1860, gratifying success, an honorarium of six *Friedrichsdor,* and something that made her no less happy, a contract for three years. But she did not stay for its duration. The management wished her to appear always in the roles of young society women, and what beginner does not dream of Gretchen and Klärchen?[55] These fine roles were held fast in the beautiful hands of Frau Versing-Hauptmann, about whose talents the Duke of Saxe-Coburg was especially enthusiastic.

It must be acknowledged in passing, however, that the management of the theatre had correctly recognized the special talents of the young beginner, as Frau von Heldburg herself later told me. Tragic and passionate roles were not those in which she could offer distinguished performances, but the play in which she could display humor, grace, and spirit, and especially womanliness—there she found her own sphere. Her Elmire in *Tartuffe* and her Beatrice in *Much Ado about Nothing,* as well as many of her spirited and charming figures in the Bauernfeld and Toepfer comedies, remain for me alive and ineffaceable. Among the classical roles her Princess in *Tasso* is said to have been outstanding. She must have been very successful in this role, for the Mannheim Theatre Commission en-gaged Oskar Begas to paint her as Lenore and presented the picture to her as a gift on her departure.

The brightness of her eyes and the melting sweetness of her voice had remained unchanged into her eightieth year, when I heard her recite occasionally lines from *Tasso* which were animated by the most profound spiritual depth. Even now the grippingly beautiful words ring in my ear: "If there were only men who knew how to value a woman's heart." What I especially remember is that charming melancholy, smiling through

---

[53] "Beautiful Hedwig" and "Heather Boys," two poems by Heinrich Heine, were set to music by the German composer, Robert Schumann (1810-1856).

[54] Nowhere does Grube give a reason for considering the role of Jane Eyre "the most effective ever written."

[55] Heroines in Goethe's plays: Gretchen, diminutive of Margarete, is the pathetic heroine in *Faust,* and Klärchen, the beloved of Egmont in the play of the same name, is one of Goethe's most delightful characters.

tears, which only a really noble nature can experience and express.

Her second position found Ellen Franz in the Court Theatre in Oldenburg, which under Moltke's direction enjoyed a very good reputation. In his chronicle of the Court Theatre, Intendant von Dalvigt makes the following evaluation of her:

1862-63. September 14. *Count Essex* . . .[56] Countess of Rutland: Frl. Ellen Franz, the role with which she entered the company of the Oldenburg Theatre. During her two years' stay, through her varied talents, she almost dominated the scene, and the list of the roles which she played during this time shows the extraordinary range of the parts she performed.

In further recognition of this artist, the author emphasizes her rare aesthetic and social characteristics, thereby coming very near the estimation I have expressed about her outstanding talents.

Two years elapse before we next see Ellen Franz on the stage; she was then playing at the National Theatre in Mannheim. In the intervening time, she had been suffering from the consequences of a fire in Frankfurt-on-the-Oder. Her first appearance there was to be her last for a long time. She was playing the Queen in *Carlos*.[57] Posa had just delivered the line, "Oh Queen, life is still beautiful . . ." when danger drew near. Fräulein Franz had already started off when a gas flame—they burned openly in those days—fanned by the draft of the descending curtain, flared up and caught her hanging sleeve; and she was surrounded by flames. Her left arm suffered such shocking burns that for two years it had to be wrapped in cotton; consequently, it was impossible even to think of a stage appearance.

In Mannheim, where she enjoyed great popularity, Herr von Bodenstedt, Intendant of the Meininger Court Theatre, was announced to her one morning.

"I was at my toilette," she related to me, "and I sent out my regrets that I could not receive him. He sent back word that I absolutely must admit him; he had to speak to me and his train left in two hours. Then I received him in God's name and with curl papers in my hair, for in those days we still wore long love locks. He made me an offer for the Meiningen Court Theatre. He knew how to speak so well about the artistic life and activity there, about the Duke's intellect and aesthetic knowledge, that he rendered me, so to speak, dumb. I signed an agreement which did not guarantee me a really substantially higher income. On the whole, I had no grounds for leaving Mannheim. I pleased the public there, and for that reason it pleased me."

To the Duke—the Lord of the stage on which she was to work—she was, however, to appear less pleasing. The young artist could in no way lay claim to beauty. On a slender body rested a well-formed head with a mouth which was not precisely small. The nose was not only very small,

---

[56]Heinrich Laube's last play, *Count Essex* (1856), is another retelling of the Elizabeth-Essex story.
[57]Schiller's *Don Carlos.*

but it also turned up. Since the skill of the photographer then was not as great as it is today, the picture that Bodenstedt showed the Duke was probably no masterpiece of photography. His Lordship remarked, "Well, this one won't be of much danger to me." But the picture had not been able to reproduce the eyes of the original, those great, wonderful, dark brown eyes from which wit and spirit flashed, in which roguishness and the greatest loving-kindness sparkled. They made no great impression on the Master of the stage when on October 20, 1867, she appeared in her first role, Julia. Indeed, the performance did not please him, a fact which is not surprising in view of what I have already said about the talents of Ellen Franz.[58]

Then, as he began to know the actress personally in the company of Bodenstedt, he began to fall under the spell of those eyes and that spirit. On the morning of March 19, 1873, the Residenz was surprised by a statement in the ducal newspaper, announcing the marriage of the Duke "with the former actress, Ellen Franz—now the Baroness von Heldburg." The emphasis on the former profession of his consort was extremely characteristic of the Duke's disposition.

The marriage ceremony took place in privacy and seclusion at the villa of the Duke in Bad Liebenstein. It cut the Gordian knot of court gossip and intrigue which had bound the relationship of the Prince and the actress. It is not worthwhile to go further into these intrigues; they missed their mark and brought about an effect just the opposite of what they had hoped. I need only mention that the father of the Duke was not far removed from the plots.

In any case, when Helene, Baroness von Heldburg, took her place at the side of her husband, the star of the Meininger began to shine.

---

[58]It has been emphasized that roles requiring grace and humor were the special forte of Ellen Franz; that of Julia in Schiller's *Fiesko* is just the opposite. She is cold, haughty, intriguing, passionate—just the characteristics which Grube says Fräulein Franz portrayed least effectively.

CHAPTER V

ARTISTIC LIFE IN MEININGEN

What Bodenstedt's fiery eloquence had related about the new artistic life in Meiningen proved to be entirely true. With the new Duke a new spirit had entered the old artistic forms. If the program had already taken on a distinguished character through the interest of the Crown Prince, it navigated under full sail into the sea of classical drama under the hand of the Duke. The 1866-67 season offered *Hamlet, Intrigue and Love,*[59] *Don Carlos, Faust, The Robbers,*[60] *Oedipus* twice, *Oedipus in Colonus* three times, then *Antigone, Lear, Medea, Iphigenia,*[61] *Emilia Galotti,*[62] *Othello, Richard III,* and *Maria Stuart.*

When we take into consideration that the theatre operated only six months of the year and that performances were given only twice weekly, we must consider the output prodigious.

The hand of the Duke was also clearly seen in the concerts of the Court Chapel. In 1866 and 1867 ten historic concerts that showed the results of well-planned effort were produced. The opera, however—since it was impossible to produce anything new with such modest means—was disbanded.

The new Intendant, "Mirza Schaffy"-Bodenstedt,[63] was then at the height of his poetical fame, and it was hoped that he would lend heightened luster to the Court Theatre. But it soon became evident that in the veins of this noted lyricist there ran no true theatre blood. He possessed no understanding of the actor's psyche, as we are accustomed to say today; repose and tranquillity, absolutely necessary for a ruler of a theatre-state, were never part of his nature. Documents give evidence that in disputes the Duke's sense of justice occasionally forced him into strong disagreement with his Intendant, but both observed the proprieties admirably. In 1870 the relationship was terminated, and Bodenstedt retired on a pension. Even if he did not come up to the Duke's expectations in all things, he had earned his reward from the Meininger by engaging Ellen Franz.

59One of Schiller's early works (1784), based on the revolutionary ideas of *Sturm und Drang.* It has held the stage to the present day.
60Written in 1781 while Schiller was still a student.
61Probably by Racine, rather than the Goethe version.
62In this prose play (1772), Lessing attacked the moral code of the nobility.
63Friedrich M. Bodenstedt (1819-1892) author, professor of Slavic languages, Intendant at Meiningen (1867-1870). His first literary success was *The Songs of Mizra Schaffy* (1851).

The Duke now became his own Intendant; and, as before, Director Karl Grabowski dispatched the theatre business. We owe to this man, too, a little place in the early history of the Meininger, partly because of his loyal completion of every duty, partly because he was such a droll figure. He was a tall, plump man with a shiny, bald head, which arched over a fine-cut countenance, made somewhat absurd by a look of the greatest self-satisfaction and exaggerated self-worth. He had a choleric manner of speaking, not unlike that of an annoyed turkey.

Mediocre playwrights think they have created a comic figure if they put a stock expression in his mouth to be used at every opportunity, suitable or unsuitable. Grabowski had such an expression; he was accustomed to cry out about everything, "Iss es de Meeglichkeit?" ["Is it possible?"]

Nowadays, no one with his meager education would be allowed to hold such an important position on any good stage. A whole multitude of Grabowski anecdotes have survived even down to the present generation of actors. As the most famous, I shall recount only his celebrated, "Meyer, didn't you hear what His Highness said? Then stand diagonal," which he thundered to an extra in the mob when the Duke, who wished the crowd to form a diagonal line, had called out to the stage, "Diagonal! Diagonal!"

But it must be acknowledged that this unusual fellow, even if only an honest stage field-sergeant, was in the business with true zeal. He knew how to train the crowd that his Field Marshal managed, and he knew how to make things lively. His directions to the actors went astray for the most part because of his grotesque manner of expression rather than in their meaning. One time he shouted to the Earth Spirit in *Faust,* who was speaking too fast: "Pause! Pause! You are a god. A god speaks in pauses." To Hans on the wall, who, in the Rütli scene is to say, "What is the priest saying? We should take an oath to Austria?" he said encouragingly, "More! More! Against the priest! You are a Protestant." This sounds very comical, but the actor understood what it meant.

That is enough of this unusual old man. To anyone who wishes to read more about his drollness, I must refer my memoirs, *Youthful Recollections of a Lucky Child.*[64] Now we must concern ourselves in detail with his successor.

On November 4, 1866, there stepped before the Meininger public for the first time a little, round, youthful comic, in the not very thankful role of Guildenstern. An agent had enticed him from the Königstädter Theater in Berlin by painting the charms of the little Residenz in attractive colors. These faded quickly as Ludwig Chronegk, the dyed-in-the-wool city dweller, stood face to face with reality. He often described to me how earnestly he wished himself elsewhere. As he had decidedly the most outstanding intelligence among the members of the company, it was no

64*Jugenderinnerungen eines Glückskindes,* Leipzig, n.d.

wonder that, when the witty Fräulein Franz appeared upon the scene the next year, these two clever people became close friends.

After Ellen Franz became Helene von Heldburg, the personnel at the beginning of the new season—the old one had ended on the day of the Duke's wedding—were somewhat surprised to learn that Herr Chronegk had been named *Régisseur.* No one believed that the jolly little man possessed the necessary earnestness for an office which carried with it so much responsibility. He had not been at all outstanding as an actor. His comic skill was not great: only in the part of a simpleton could he give a really delightful performance, and, dressed as a woman, he was funny and decent, even graceful. I can still see him in the one-act farce, *The False Cataloni,* in which he danced, sang falsetto, and threw himself a bouquet, for which he thanked himself with deep bows and forced smiles. All this was very funny.

His artistic training was such that he did not seem especially prepared to become a director on a stage which emphasized classical drama. Then, too, no one had ever perceived in him any special zeal. "Always jolly," he was a good social companion and a willingly ridiculous comic; and it must be admitted that on the stage he was always prepared. He never, as so many comics like to do, tempted the other actors to laugh or to make sport of others. So it was with reason that his colleagues accepted this appointment with thoughtful head shaking. Only the clever Weilenbeck[65] saw in Chronegk more than the others.

But to whom God gives an office, He also gives understanding. And his former colleague (now the Baroness von Heldburg) had been correct in her opinion of the little comic's hidden character. To be sure, his literary education was not great; at the beginning of a rehearsal of *Nathan,* he could call out: "Let's go! Who has the first speech?" [66] He liked to speak with a decided Berlin accent, although he could, of course, express himself in faultless High German whenever it suited him.

His superior qualities far outweighed his deficiencies. He had a clear understanding which quickly found the most natural and complete solution for all questions of production and scenery. He had a talent for making clear to the actor in short, striking phrases—often in drastic but easily understood ways—what the central idea of a role was; he could demonstrate a part, something which is beyond many of the little "Latin" directors of our day. He possessed an incredibly powerful endurance for work and the greatest business cleverness; above all, he displayed an energy which occasionally degenerated into a lack of consideration and rudeness. He had the gift of forcefully impressing the actors, a gift which does not come easily to directors of short stature. It is easier to command looking down from above than looking up from below.

---

65 Josef Weilenbeck was one of Meiningen's finest actors; in a later chapter Grube discusses his performances at length.

66 Lessing's *Nathan the Wise* was such a standard German classic that Grube uses this example to point up Chronegk's literary deficiency.

In addition, he did not lack personal courage. For instance, during one of the guest engagements the stagehands—whom he usually managed in a friendly manner, but whom he occasionally had to rebuke sharply—began to grumble and to complain that they would take the whole matter to the Privy Councillor. After a performance he went to the cafe where the crew gathered and sat down among them. Naturally nothing happened to him and the whole thing was reduced to a tempest in a teapot. This was very important, for if the Meininger stagehands had struck (the word "strike" was, of course, unknown at that time; mostly one heard of such things only from England), it would have been impossible to find substitutes. No stagehands, unfamiliar with their machinery, no matter how skillful they were, could have found their way in the complicated apparatus. The performances would have become simply impossible.

Beyond all praise was the staunch devotion which he dedicated to his Duke: he was a true servant, a Fridolin.[67] I shall never forget the appearance of that little man, muffled up in a blanket, crippled with arthritis, with hands speckled with iodine—in those days people considered iodine an efficacious remedy against this disease—and forbidden by his doctors to leave his bed, who would not for any price let the important rehearsals for the guest performances in Berlin out of his control.

We must acknowledge Chronegk's responsibility for much of the glory which the name "Meininger" calls to life. He was the first to realize that in Meiningen had been created a great work of art which should not be hidden in a little Residenz, but should be shown in the capital city. His innate business sense recognized at the same time that only through the great revenue presumably to be gained by such an engagement could the money be raised to carry out expensive productions at Meiningen, for which in the long run even the ducal purse would not be sufficient. Chronegk's special contribution to the Meininger lay in the organization and execution of the guest tours. How much astuteness and business ability were necessary to conclude the often complicated contracts, especially with foreign theatres! And then to put the large, many-branched artistic body into motion! In foreign countries it was especially difficult to train the extras who had to be added to fill up the stage. It was exceedingly hard to give them any notion of how they were to act and what movements they should assume within the framework of the play.

Only a person experienced in the theatre can fully understand the whole compass of these enormous difficulties. He could truly say of himself, "I am consumed by serving."[68] The overtaxing strains on his spiritual as well as his physical powers did not allow this untiring man to become old. During the guest engagement at Düsseldorf in June 1886, he broke down, but it was only a light stroke. A guest appearance in America, for which

---

67St. Fridolin was a sixth century Irish missionary to the Upper Rhine. He built several chapels and was known for his industry and fidelity to his work. Since everything known about him is contained in one account, some historians believe him to be a legendary character.
68"Inserviendo consumnor."

arrangements had been nearly completed, had to be abandoned; and in the fall the Duke decided to put off the other guest tours that had been planned for that year. His gallant field lieutenant recovered enough to continue, although the eighty-first guest appearance in Odessa, in 1890, was to be his last; the Duke wished to spare his faithful worker the pain of seeing a successor in his place. On June 19, 1891, Chronegk succumbed in his fifty-third year to the heart ailment which had pained him for many years.

These words adorn the stone sarcophagus which covers his resting place in the Jewish Cemetery in Meiningen:

GEORG, DUKE OF SAXE-MEININGEN,
AND HELENE, BARONESS VON HELDBURG,
TO THEIR FRIEND

CHAPTER VI

THE REHEARSAL PERIOD IN MEININGEN

A remarkable artistic trinity had now been effected: a ruling Prince, a former actress, and a Jew. And it was indeed truly a *trinity,* for almost never did a difference of opinion arise, except, of course, about things that were tried on the stage. With such cordial co-operation a division of labor was established—though only in the most general terms.

The Duke, in whose hands the supervision obviously remained, determined the outlines of the production and the forms of the presentation; Chronegk worked out the details; and Frau von Heldburg took as her province everything of a really dramatic nature. For the most part, she proposed the plays to be produced, and she was responsible for the masterly adaptations of the texts. Under the title *Theater der Meininger,* these were printed by the publishing house of von Grumbkow, which is no longer functioning, and later by Conrad. They are now so seldom seen, at least in the full set, that they now belong only to the bibliophile. In addition, she began to work as mistress of speech.

Although her new life smiled upon her, it was only with profound sorrow that she sacrificed her art to her love. She remained with all her soul an actress. When the Duke lay ill in peril of his life, his mother, who naturally did not feel friendly toward her middle-class daughter-in-law, asked what her future would be if the worst happened. Without thinking, she answered, "Why then, I would certainly return to the theatre."

The ducal mother, who must have been expecting quite another answer —probably a little appeal to the goodness of the noble house—thereupon remarked, "My dear, one can be too proud."

Helene von Heldburg found a substitute for her own career in her efforts to impart to others something of her own ability and knowledge. The Meiningen court was not in a position to pay noted guest artists. This was not merely a question of money, but rather a fear that one powerful talent might destroy the ensemble, the goal toward which everything was aimed. It was absolutely forbidden that an actor attempt to force his way out of the artistic frame to individual prominence. The Duke hated the airs of the star; in them he rightly saw the destruction of the stage. His aim was to add good actors to the ensemble without distorting the stage picture. It was not unusual that some famous artist would be brought in for a guest performance: Barnay, Robert, Dettmer, Mitterwurzer, Anna Haverlandt,

Pauline Ulrich, and others; but they had to adapt themselves to the Meininger production methods. In no way might they conduct themselves as stars. As a demonstration of his aversion to the star system, the Duke did not permit his visitors to perform as *guests;* they were designated as "honorary members" of the company, and therefore, became part of the rank and file of the Meininger, although in a somewhat elevated place.

Frau von Heldburg worked devotedly in her position as mistress of speech. I do not say as a teacher, for it must be truthfully said that it was not her aim to promote her own artistic style; her own individuality was too pronounced for that. She could not—or would not—intrude on the characteristic features of an individual talent. Rather, she sought to make the pupil her speaking tube, as it were.

It is a remarkable fact, but one often observed, that some truly artistic people cannot be independently creative—partly because of insufficient intelligence, partly because of a deficient education. Yet these same persons can surrender themselves entirely to outside direction. Unlike persons of real talent, who want to work independently and will always rebel against close direction, they welcome having a role interpreted for them. The most remarkable thing about these carefully directed talents is that their performances do not appear as such; they give the impression that the fruits grew in their own gardens. With actors and actresses of this sort much work was done in Meiningen, and with much success. What hymns of praise have been sung to many an actor and actress which rightly belong to Frau von Heldburg. It should not go unnoticed, however, that many of those about whom we have been speaking, through industry and improvement in education, have achieved independence and have later filled distinguished places in noted theatres.

The Meininger counted among its members many individual artists, who, if not of the first rank, were certainly highly qualified performers. They will be discussed fully at a later date.

Although the type of instruction that Frau von Heldburg practiced can hardly be represented as suitable for universal procedure, it was exactly correct for the aims and goals of the Meininger. Even the very smallest roles were carried to the highest perfection, and above everything else there was achieved a unity of production that only the Meininger could attain in those days.

A three-headed direction! That must certainly have made the rehearsal periods difficult, for during rehearsals it is indispensable that a determined will pull everything together and decide on a single effect. The Duke took this decisive role, of course, but I cannot remember that he ever gave an important instruction without the concurrence of his co-workers. If a difference of opinion arose, the scene in question would be rehearsed according to each interpretation. It was not unusual to see it in three versions. Then the most effective parts would be chosen from each, or without hesitation the version to be retained would be chosen.

It should be pointed out that there was never a so-called Book of Direction, the *Regiebuch*. Everything was planned, so to speak, from event to event. Such a procedure cost a great deal of time, but in Meiningen time always played just as small a part as gold. I need hardly stress, though, that the Duke never lost sight of fundamental principles.

The length of the rehearsals, beginning about five or six and seldom ending before midnight, was never computed beforehand. Once the Duke called, "I wish all the members a Happy New Year." It was New Year's Eve! Then the rehearsal resumed. Even the longest rehearsal was never broken for a supper pause for the company. In a good middle-class way the Duke would bring a sandwich out of a paper bag, and sometimes his wife would bring him some hot chocolate. After the rehearsal the princely couple took their evening meal in the castle, and then remained up longer discussing the evening's work.

At the beginning of rehearsals, the members arrived with the greatest punctuality; it was a matter of course that no one wished to be guilty of arriving late. The company met in the orchestra, and Chronegk usually took the stage; he always did for a first rehearsal. No one ever saw the traditional director's table and chair; they were superfluous when there was no *Regiebuch*.

As I have already remarked, Chronegk knew how to make it very plain to the actors what the Duke wanted, and he knew, too, how to interpret these desires to them. Frequently both were necessary, for the Duke was not familiar with stage vocabulary, and he was always under the spell of the poetry or of a special role. For example, he did not say to the actor, "Go to the right or the left." Instead, he would say to Max, "Now you find yourself drawn to Wallenstein." Often misunderstandings were increased by the Duke's faulty enunciation. Both of these peculiarities of the princely director often caused the drollest misunderstandings.

Once a young woman, not familiar with the Duke's ways, was cast as Berta von Bruneck.[69] The Duke had directed the scene with Rudenz in the rocky gorge so that Berta sat on a rock while Rudenz, leaning on his spear, stood before her. That made a better picture than when both stood side by side, a posture that seemed very awkward in so small a setting. A professional director would have said at this point, "Now, dear Fräulein, sit down!" But in the spirit of the role, the Duke called, "You are tired."

"But no, by no means, Your Highness," the girl answered eagerly, for she thought the Duke heard weariness in her voice. Then he said, "You are coming from the hunt."

The lady replied, "Excuse me, Highness, no! From Coburg."

Another time the same scene gave rise to a much more comical misunderstanding. The Duke called to Rudenz—if I'm not mistaken, it was my handsome namesake, Karl Grube. For a moment Grube stood evidently at a loss; then excitedly and abruptly, he hurried off the stage.

---

[69] In Schiller's *William Tell* (1804).

Chronegk naturally called after him, "What's the matter? Have you gone out of your mind?"

"No, Mr. Director, I'll stand a good deal, but that goes too far. That I cannot allow to be said to me."

"What was it?"

"You heard yourself what His Highness plainly said to me."

"But what was it?"

"He called out to me in front of everybody, 'You played that like a sow.' "[70]

But the Duke had really called out, "You have a boar spear." Rudenz had forgotten that he was supposed to carry on a hunting spear, a boar pike.

Much weight was placed on the insistence that from the first rehearsal all properties were to be present on stage—a very useful requirement which even today the best theatres are not always able to fulfill.

The serious historian will glance at me disapprovingly but I cannot refrain from relating a little joke—not only because of the humor—but because it sheds a characteristic light. After all, it is a story about a light! In Act I, scene 3 of *The Ancestress*,[71] the steward was to appear with a light. Armed with this, Emil Pückert, a very skillful actor, but a very nervous one, stood at the first rehearsal directly behind the door and waited for his cue. And he waited and waited and waited for the time to enter. Finally, from out front came the voice of the Duke, "Herr Pückert, you should be entering with a flaming light."

Somewhat offended, Herr Pückert extended his light. How surprised he was as he saw that there was no light—the candle had burned entirely down. He had waited two hours, for it had taken that long to rehearse the first two scenes. These cover only eleven pages in the Cotta version.

With the same attention to detail, the proper scenery and furniture had to be in place at the first rehearsal. This had the disadvantage that any alterations, brought about by continuing changes, necessitated the dragging back and forth of heavy chairs, tables, cupboards, and plasterwood chimneys. Such intervals are normally not disagreeable to the straining actors; but if they last too long, such breaks enervate the actors, making them impatient and irritable. As an advantage, this plan offered to the director the priceless opportunity of having the complete picture before his eyes from the beginning, while it offered the actor the opportunity of putting himself in the place he was later to bring to life.

Richard III can swagger and preen himself on the throne which he has obtained so painfully in quite a different manner than is possible on a farmer's chair, which is usually used for rehearsal. The word "indicates" was entirely unknown at Meininger rehearsals. Every artist was required to rehearse his role with the same vocal strength and spiritual depth that he would use on the evening of performance. Even if the scene in which he

---

[70]The misunderstanding rested on two words *sauspielen*—to act like a sow and *sauspiess* —a boar pike.
[71]By Franz Grillparzer (1791-1872), leading Austrian playwright of the nineteenth century.

appeared was rehearsed four or five times, he was not permitted to relax, just as the director did not. Neither the Duke or his wife, nor Chronegk, ever seemed to experience fatigue. Even if a play had been produced once, or even several times, the rehearsals were conducted as if a new piece were being prepared.

When a play is first put on the boards, as one says in the theatre: the production stands! That means: now the scenery, the lighting, the costumes, in short, all technical matters as well as the interpretation of the roles, the placing of the actors, the speeches, and the timing of the different scenes are set for all time; no amount of repetition introduces any variation. Rehearsals take place only when a new cast demands them; then, the actor who has just joined the cast must fit into an already set pattern. In major theatres, since the whole production rests strictly on a promptbook, differences of opinion are out of the question. Of course, this promptbook is different from the one which the director had worked out in advance and which was altered many times during the rehearsals.

In Meiningen a play "stood" only in its broadest outlines; in other respects, it was in a state of constant change. Whatever was found good and workable was practiced more and more in new rehearsals until it was set. Whatever was inadequate served as a basis for new efforts.

As a rule, orders, rather than suggestions, were given by those in charge, as is more or less the case on every well-run stage; nevertheless, suggestions by the players were never ignored. Whoever believed that he had hit upon a good idea could take it to Chronegk, or for that matter, directly to the Duke. If it seemed a good one, the idea would be subjected to a test at once.

For example, in the death scene of Talbot[72] the Duke had provided a stuffed horse [Plate V A], since he believed that on the battlefield there should be dead horses as well as the corpses of men. As the colossus was placed on the stage, Frau von Heldburg and Chronegk raised serious objections: this unusual sight would divert the eyes of the audience from the actors, especially since the animal was covered with a white battle blanket. All feasible positions for placing the huge body on the stage were tried. The farther it was shoved into the background, the more conspicuous it became. A darker cover probably would have avoided this danger—why no one had hit upon it, I cannot say; probably the Duke wanted that entirely white patch in the picture.

Then I ventured to remark that a possible solution to this dilemma would be for the horse not to be placed by itself in a particular spot; instead, it could be related to the principal person of the scene. It should be Talbot's warhorse, which had been struck down by the same cannonball as he. Immediately my proposal was accepted. The horse was placed with its back to the audience, its head to the ground, its hind legs on a raised level of the stage. At the beginning of the scene, I was pulled forward from underneath the horse by the soldiers; then it served as a support for my

---

[72] In Schiller's *The Maid of Orleans* (1802).

back. Thus came about one of the most individual scenes of the Meininger. The thought of completing the picture of the battlefield through only one fallen horse must have been in the Duke's mind for some time. A sketch of a scene in *The Battle of Arminius,* drawn in 1875, had shown a dead horse, as can be seen from the illustration in this volume. [Plate V B]

But the Directors did not notice the suggestions of only the featured players. Shortly after I joined the Meininger as a beginning actor, I received a little legacy that made possible a fairly long stay in Paris. In the productions of *The Imaginary Invalid* and *The Learned Ladies* at the Théâtre-Français I was struck by some nuances which the Meininger productions lacked. I described them to Frau von Heldburg, and soon the little twenty-four-year old actor received a personally written thank-you letter and a notice that the suggestions had been tried out and were being incorporated into the plays.

The Duke himself now and then questioned the younger members of the group when there were difficulties in finding the correct solution to a scene: "Come now! Hasn't anyone of you a reasonable suggestion?" One time this cost him dearly. They were trying desperately to doctor the castle courtyard scene in *Fiesko,* but with no success.

In those days, the applause of the audience was a test of excellence, and acclamation in the middle of scenes—now something long regarded as disturbing and tasteless—was then in vogue. If the speech of the Knight Raoul, as well as that of Kosinski, did not bring a round of applause, the actors could feel that they had failed and might as well go bury themselves. For the most part, it is true that classical plays, especially those of Schiller, are "fashioned for applause." Such bids for public approbation were made in Meiningen, too, with perfectly legitimate means, of course. But at the conclusion of Act IV, scene 10, these legitimate means failed completely. Fiesko is supposed to say lightly and negligently, with no emphasis, "Now go inside, and taste my Cyprian wine." He said it; nothing happened. Then again with particular stress, as if the words had a deeper meaning; nothing happened! The nobles in the scene became very excited, but quite in vain!

We had in our midst at that time an Austrian Jew, who because of his dry wit was very popular with us.

"Now, just watch me," he said to some of the other actors, as Chronegk was standing in his vicinity and could hear him. "I know what the scene lacks."

Like a hawk, Chronegk pounced upon him. "Man, if you have an idea, why didn't you say so? Speak up! What does the Fourth Act need?"

"Applause, Herr Director!"

As the guest tours became more and more extended—they finally lasted from six to eight months—the plays, although they remained subject to continual improvement, became somewhat set. The methods of production, however, were never put into writing, a fact which today is greatly to be deplored.

The most accurate knowledge of every play and of each part was alive in the whole Meininger Company. Whenever a new actor joined the group, the director scarcely needed to give him any directions; they would be whispered to him from all sides. This was not only the result of many rehearsals and performances; it sprang from the most zealous interest, which every Meininger cherished for the whole. Each one felt himself—no matter how small his role, even if it was only the smallest—as a necessary and indispensable part of the whole artistic work. A strong tradition had been built up which each one was proud to preserve. It is impossible to describe adequately the pride of community feeling which animated the Meininger.

In this association of colleagues, there disappeared the class ranks which in those days sharply divided the principal actors from the "little players." The group participation which placed the heroes next to the bit players equalized everything; all thought of themselves only as Meininger.

It is well known that the Meininger made their reputation mainly through their folk and mass scenes on which the greatest attention was lavished at rehearsals. Since that time we have seen a greater concentration on mass scenes in the theatre; I recall the productions in Reinhardt's theatre, that circus that was just as favorable to mob scenes as it was destructive to individual performances. I accord the greatest recognition to this master, but even in the finest shadings in the mass scenes, he did not surpass the Meininger. That has not been possible, nor will it be; because the masses were not produced by "supers," but, instead, by young artists—gifted beginners—men and women.

Even this was not enough; every member of the company was obliged to work as an extra. *Mitmachen* [co-operation] does not adequately express this—rank and salary, although both might be significant, allowed no exception. Whenever they had no part in the play, the first hero and the first heroine had to stand beside the untrained beginner in the bustling throng of the folk. As we may well understand, these methods were not at first acceptable, but the longer an artist remained with the Meininger, the more he perceived that on this groundwork of equality, the whole structure of the Meininger was erected and maintained.

Besides, everyone knew that the eye of the Duke rested upon every "super" with the same interest as on the stars. Even if confidential backstage talk designated the Duke as "the old man with the long grey beard," he exercised on everyone all the charm that surrounds a great personality. Each one revered him as a private reveres his general on the field of battle. Anyone who could carry off praise from him was extremely happy, and he bestowed praise or blame on the least of the Roman mob in the same way as he did on Brutus or Marc Antony.

How great an emphasis was laid upon the "extras"—their interdependence in the action on which the "silent miming" rested—is best shown by the fact that without any hesitation the Duke allowed von Bülow his requested release when the Concert Master threatened to resign unless his wife, an excellent and spirited actress, should be relieved from serving as an extra. For what reasons von Bülow wished to leave Meiningen, I never knew, but he certainly knew how to lay hold of the Duke at a place where yielding was impossible. One exception would have brought about the destruction of the whole system. I have heard from the Duke's own lips how deeply it affected him to give up von Bülow.

Paul Lindau has rendered us a great service in collecting a large number of the directions which he received from the Duke during the time he was Intendant.[73] I think that in these rules of staging all that is characteristic in the art of the Meininger is set forth. We must, however, remember that the idea of the picturesque in that day was entirely different from ours. Painting had not yet approached the laws of architecture. Nothing appeared more objectionable than symmetry and parallelism—*tempora mutantur.*

Through his critical ability, as well as through his dramatic talent, Lindau was well acquainted with the theatre; this brilliant, spirited man had theatre blood in his veins. He quickly found that he was in the right place in his new office. He produced in Meiningen, as later in Berlin, many fine presentations; yet in many ways he was still a *homo novus.* The Duke, who after every performance was accustomed to write an exceedingly detailed letter to his Intendant and Director, found that he was obliged to comment on things with which Chronegk and his successor, Paul Richard, had been thoroughly familiar. Through Lindau's article in an issue of the *Deutsche Bühne,* the official publication of the German Stage Union, we are able to trace out in the main the production principles of the Duke, stated in his own words:

> We should take into consideration in the composition of a stage picture that the middle of the scene does not correspond with the middle of the stage. If the composition proceeds from the geometric middle, two halves result. From this the danger follows that in the arrangement of groups, disposing them to the right and left will result in a somewhat symmetrical balance. This will appear wooden, stiff, and boring.
>
> (The charm of Japanese art rests on the avoidance of all symmetry. "L'ennui naquit un jour de l'uniformité," said Boileau about artistic creation in general. In plastic art "uniformity," which the French esthete pointed out as the mother of tedium, is called symmetry.)
>
> The exception confirms the rule. A composition with the principal figure or the principal group centered, with the subordinate figures or groups standing on each side at more or less regular intervals can be justified artistically on the stage, if

---

73 At Meiningen 1895-1899.

one aspires to present a solemnly austere—one might even say ascetic—impression. The Sistine Madonna of Raphael is an example that comes readily to mind. Such a picture always has the character of serenity. But the principal requirement of the stage is to reveal motion and the impetuous progress of action; therefore, in general, this arrangement is to be avoided, since it is stiff and retards the impression of movement.

It is seldom good to have anything stand in the middle of the stage. It is practical to set movable or other scenery to one of the sides, naturally at a distance from the wings so that it can be easily seen by those sitting in the auditorium.

The actor should at no time stand in the middle of the stage directly in front of the prompt box, but instead he should always stand a little to the right or the left of the prompter. The middle of the stage, reckoned as about as wide as the prompt box and extending from the footlights to the perspective in the background, should serve for the actor only as a passageway from right to left, or vice versa. He has no business there for any other reason. It is also best, if possible, to avoid having two persons standing at an exact distance from the prompt box.

More attention should be paid to a pleasing relationship between the actors' positions and the set decorations. It is a widely current misconception in directing that in the relationship of the actor to the architecture, no attention need be paid to the perspective of the painted trees, buildings, etc.

It is true that some mistakes cannot be avoided when the living forms of the actors, unchangeable in size, become proportionately too large with every step backwards into the sharp perspective of the painted settings. But if they can appear to diminish in size, then the disturbing effect will disappear. For example, an actor should not approach the scenery in the upstage wings so closely that the disproportion becomes striking. He should not—as one often sees—stand immediately in front of a painted house, the door of which reaches up to his hips, where he, without stretching, can look into a window on the second floor, and where, if he raised his hand, he could touch the chimney.

The scenic pieces toward which the actor moves must always be approximately in the same proportion to a man as real ones would be. As an example, the temple in *Iphigenia in Tauris* should be placed toward the front of the stage, so that its tall columns rise upward to the flies and tower over the human figures. It does not matter if those in the audience cannot see the top of the temple building. Indeed, it is really more pleasing if they can see part of the entablature over the columns, the supporting beams, and a portion of the dome, while the remainder of the dome can be hidden in the greenery of the foliage borders.

The balcony of *Romeo and Juliet* is usually placed much too low. There is one disadvantage that in a really correct placement of the balcony, Juliet stands somewhat high, but that is less important than the customary mistake—that with a balcony of moderate height, there is always one disturbing thought: Even if he were not a really good gymnast, Romeo could with only one leap reach his "inaccessible" sweetheart and fold her in his arms.

The actors must never lean against the painted scenery (columns and the like). If the movement is vigorous, the contact will shake the painted piece and any illusion is lost. Yet if the actor uses the necessary caution not to joggle the canvas scenery with his movements, this lack of freedom restricts his actions until they are offensive in their rigidity.

Scenic pieces against which an actor may lean or upon which he can support himself (such as door frames, tree trunks, etc.) must be made of sturdy materials and must be solid (as indeed is becoming the usual practice in the better theatres).[74]

With the simultaneous use of painted and three-dimensional objects on the stage, all possible care must be taken so that the differences in these materials are not readily apparent. The shading, for example, from real or artificial flowers and leaves to those which are openly painted must be so finely achieved that the audience can scarcely distinguish the painted from the real. (It is absolutely inartistic, even absurd, if, for example, on a rose-bush the one rose which is to be plucked is the only plastic one among many painted ones; or if one sees on the rear elevation in the workshop of *The Violin Maker of Cremona* a half-dozen painted violins with painted shadows and among them a real violin which is to be used and so is three-dimensional with real shadows. Besides producing an unreal effect in relation to the painted violins, the one real one seems to be much too large, almost the size of a viola.)

The attempts to bring the human figure into harmony with the architecture at the back of the stage—for example, using on the scaffolds of the Fortress of Uri in *Tell* the figures of children in appropriate costumes and masks as laborers, representing adults working at a distance—cannot be said to be successful. The carriage of boys is plainly quite different from that of adults. In addition, the blending of contours and the shading of hues, which nature would achieve by distance and which can be reproduced by painting, are not attained by the living figures in the background. The living form shows a more sharply etched clarity than the painted surroundings, and the eyes of the viewer do not see working adults made small by distance, but little gnomelike creatures, dwarfs, with faces painted to look old.

---

[74]The parentheses in this section are Grube's.

Borders made of cut strips of linen painted blue to represent the sky (called in stage slang "ozone rags") and running cross-wise above the stage must never be used. In scenes depicting country landscapes, trees with widely extending boughs may be employed. These extended arches can usually be used for town scenes, streets, and market places, too. Sometimes the action presents a place in such a way that above the streets and squares garlands or banners, flags or pennants, can be stretched. If this is impractical and the sky must appear above the scene, even then cloud borders are preferable to the painted blue linen. There is no place in an artistically decorated set for this tediously ugly blue border.

At the first rehearsal of a new play with crowd scenes and a large personnel, the hair of the director usually stands on end. He almost despairs of the possibility of enlivening and molding the stiff, inflexible mass. A great help in solving this problem is to have the scenery up permanently from the very beginning. Any change in the setting, such as hanging or shifting scenery or moving furniture during rehearsals slows them terribly, upsets the nerves, and wearies and enervates the actors.[75]

In costume plays everything should be tested as early as possible with the weapons, helmets, armor, swords, etc. Then during the play the actors will not be hindered in their actions by the unfamiliarity and ponderous weight of the weapons.

In these plays it is essential even before dress rehearsal, which should differ from the opening performance only in the absence of the public, that the artists should rehearse in costume—either the proper one or, if this is not yet ready or must be kept fresh, in one of corresponding cut. For several rehearsals before the dress rehearsal, the actors must wear headdresses, cloaks, trains, etc., either exactly like or somewhat like those to be worn on opening night. The actor should encounter nothing unforeseen or surprising at the time of performance. He should be given the opportunity to make himself at home in the unfamiliar costume of the past. The viewers should not perceive in his entrance and actions that he is wearing a costume which a wardrobe man has just put on him; they should not be reminded of a costume ball or a masquerade.

Carriage and movement are influenced by different costumes and modes. In the costume of an earlier period, from ancient times to the Renaissance, an actor cannot assume our present manner of standing with heels together, the required stance in our society for both the military man and the civilian. This way of standing, heel to heel, seems to have come into universal use

[75]Not until late in his career after much experience with staging methods did the Duke recognize this. (Grube's footnote.)

no earlier than the dance step of the minuet. A leader of the Mercenaries would not stand as an *abbé galant* of the eighteenth century nor as a modern second lieutenant with feet close together. The natural, correct, and most pleasing manner of standing in any costume up to the eighteenth century is straddle-legged, with one foot placed ahead of the other. A general rule is this: for the most part everything parallel on the stage is to be avoided. This is especially true in costume plays.

Spears, halberds, lances, etc., should never be carried in a straight, upward position as are the muskets and swords of our present day infantry and cavalry. In the handling of old weapons, discretion must prevail: they should not be held at the same distance from each other, nor in exact formation. Here they should be pulled together, there spread farther apart, and held not perpendicularly, but obliquely and crosswise.

Every helmet, except the antique, must be set so low on the forehead that only the muscles above the eyebrow are visible. The popular manner, placing the helmet at the back of the head and down on the neck, is the way of the tenor, but is not suitable for the theatre. Our gentlemen in costume probably fear that if they wear their helmets properly, they will disarrange their curly locks; but we're not concerned with that.

It is a real mistake to place the actors in positions parallel to one another. If it is necessary to place groups parallel to the footlights, then a direct face-to-face position is not attractive; this is especially true when two actors of the same height stand parallel to the footlights. If the actor has to move from the right to the left, he should avoid moving directly across; that is not the best way on the stage. Instead, he should move unobtrusively at an angle to break the straight line.

If three or more actors in a scene are on the stage at the same time, they should avoid above all else standing in a straight line. They should always stand at an angle. The distances between the individual actors should not be equal. If they stand at equal intervals, they will become uninteresting and as lifeless as figures on a chessboard. It is always attractive if the actor can unaffectedly touch a piece of furniture or some other suitable object on the stage. This gives the appearance of life and naturalness.

If the stage has different levels—steps, hilly ground with rocks, and the like—the actor should not let the opportunity escape to display a harmonious line by making his movements rhythmical. He should also, for example, when ascending a flight of steps, avoid standing on one step with both feet at the same time. If he climbs down from an elevation and has to stop to say something or to make an observation, he should place one foot a little lower than the other. By this, his whole body gains in freedom and attractiveness. "One leg high" is the usual command from the director in this instance.

The management of masses on the stage demands special and different attention during rehearsal. There is hardly a theatre capable of casting from its own company all the extras essential for a large folk scene. Besides the members of the chorus and the so-called house supers, whom the really skillful and experienced actors might join, workers in even greater numbers must be drawn for the *komparserie* [supers], the untrained masses for whom this is just extra work and for whom each rehearsal and each performance is paid at an agreed rate. Among these people, who change often and whom the director cannot know, many times one finds those available who can be trained, who can understand what the director says, and who are not awkward in the performances. But along with such people, there are many to whom nothing can be taught and whose appearance is very comical. Often they want to play in their own manner and can cause a great deal of harm.

It is the business of the director and the stage manager subordinate to him to discover quickly the especially capable and the especially incapable and to separate the sheep from the goats, so that the dubious ones can be put in as fillers where they can do no harm.

The extras should be divided into smaller groups, each of which is separately trained. Each of these groups should be led by a skilled, thoroughly trained actor or by a clever member of the chorus, who "covers" the others and who, therefore, stands conspicuously in the foreground. To some extent, this leader must carry the responsibility that subordinates entrusted to him obey the orders he gives. He himself is responsible to the director for such subordinates and must see to it that positions, movements, etc., will be produced on cue. These leaders receive partial scripts with cues, in which the directions are often only generally given by the author as "noise," "tumult," "murmurs," "cries," "shrieks," and the like; these the director has to put into words to be committed to memory by the performers. Such insertions must naturally be presented in different forms and must not be given simultaneously by all the groups in the same manner.

The problems which devolve upon the leader of a group of walk-ons are not simple. It is a regrettable error and one very harmful to artistic efforts when members of the company engaged as "actors" consider these roles valueless and unworthy of real artists, and try to avoid them whenever possible; or if they are required to play such parts, they make no effort to hide their disinclination.

In Meiningen all artists without exception are required to do duty as extras. (It was this practice that achieved the amazing effect at the first appearance of the Meininger, for the genuine interplay of the crowd contrasted remarkably with the awkward stiffness and apathy of the walk-ons to which audiences had long been accustomed.)

The lack of beauty resulting from poor placement of individual artists in relation to one another is especially disturbing in crowd scenes. The principal charm of grouping lies in a beautiful line of actors' heads. Just as uniformity of carriage is to be avoided, absolute uniformity in the height of those placed next to each other is to be avoided. If it occurs that several of the same height are placed together, then they should stand on different levels. Depending on the situation, some might kneel, some stand, some bend over, others remain erect. It works out very well if an irregular semi-circle can be built around the person or the object on which the gaze of the group is fixed.

The director must also insure that all those standing nearest the audience, and therefore most prominently in the eyes of the audience, be placed and arranged so that their shoulders are not all at the same angle to the footlights. It should be impressed upon every extra that he must alter his position if he notices he is standing in exactly the same position as his neighbor. In no well-composed picture would one find many figures standing together at the same height and in the same position. This order should be repeated to the actors and extras at almost every rehearsal of the mob scenes, because they always forget it.

The extras must be forcefully instructed not to look out into the audience. It is natural that they should do this; for many, "play-acting" is new and unusual, and it excites their curiosity to look into the dark auditorium.

Action that is not really attractive—for example, dragging off the dead and wounded—must be "covered" and thus be hidden as much as possible from the eyes of the audience. But this should not be done in such a way that a thick and impenetrable wall of men hides the action; that is ridiculous. The masking should be somewhat spotty; the viewer should not see everything that is happening, but he should see enough so that he can surmise what the action is all about.

To give the impression that a very large crowd of folk is on the stage, groups should be so arranged that those standing on the edge of the group extend into the wings. From no place in the auditorium should anyone see the edge of the crowd. To the members of the audience it should be believable that farther off stage still more of the crowd are thronging.

CHAPTER VII

COSTUMES AND PROPERTIES

Next to the crowd scenes the "authenticity" of the Meininger—the historical accuracy of costumes, weapons, furniture, and properties—aroused general admiration. In this they were not originators, but rather refiners; for attempts had been made earlier to present, instead of the fantastic and conventional theatre costumes, those really suitable to the "time" in which the play is laid.

About the middle of the eighteenth century the opera singer, Madame Favart, had tried to place on the Parisian stage peasant women no longer dressed in silk skirts, high-heeled shoes, and jewels; instead, she showed them in peasant clothing—although it was somewhat idealized. Later the famous Clairon and Lekain[76] attempted to replace the hoop skirt and elaborate wig by introducing Roman costume. Their attempts were not crowned with success, for they alone appeared in antique costumes, while their co-workers remained true to their traditional theatre costume.

In Germany the reform was more effective; Koch[77] in Leipzig was in the forefront of this movement. At the opening of the Schauspielhaus on October 6, 1766, he presented Elias Schlegel's *The Battle of Arminius*[78] in costumes which were praised by his contemporaries as "most correct." This same manager, too, displayed courage in introducing *Götz* to the Berlin stage. Koch's costumes, designed by the Director of the Academy, Meil, suggested sixteenth-century styles. However, one should not conclude from the numerous magazine articles—which at first praised the magnificence of the "clothes," as well as acknowledging their correctness—that these costumes were really historically correct. For what was typically used for all plays not set in ancient times was a costume which approximated somewhat the sixteenth-century Spanish dress. The well-known etchings of Chodowiecki[79] prove this.

Not until the beginning of the nineteenth century did Moritz, Count von

---

[76]This remarkable pair, both protégés of Voltaire, were among the great French actors of the eighteenth century. Claire de Latude (1723-1803) adopted the stage name of Mlle. Clairon, and Lekain's real name was Henri Louis Cain (or Kain) (1729-1788).

[77]Heinrich Koch (b. 1703) started his career with Karolina Neuber as actor, translator, and scene painter. He repaid her by cheating her out of her acting patent when she was an old woman.

[78]Not to be confused with the later, better-known *Battle of Arminius* by von Kleist which was performed by the Meininger.

[79]Daniel Nikolaus Chodowiecki (1726-1801), German painter and engraver. Among the books for which he designed illustrations are Schiller's *The Robbers*, Cervantes' *Don Quixote*, and Shakespeare's works.

Brühl, Intendant of the Berlin Court Theatre, attempt to introduce historically correct costuming. Yet from his published sketches, it seems evident that his research was in many cases superficial or that he interpreted the sources poorly. In the pictures of the feminine roles the appearance of a short bodice strikingly indicates how much the artist consciously or unconsciously showed admiration for the style of his own time.

Through Brühl's action people began to take notice of costuming appropriate to different centuries and to disregard the costume practices of the old wardrobe masters. Theatre wits characterized their methods with the amusing saying: "Before Christ, everyone wore leggings; after Christ, knights' boots." It is true that boots played a great role after the appearance of *Wallenstein.*[80] In 1870 in Breslau, I saw *Othello* performed in Wallenstein costumes. A famous picture of Dessoir in the title role of this tragedy furnishes proof that even at the Berlin Schauspielhaus it was set in the seventeenth century.

In general, the theatre possessed five stock sets of costumes: antique, medieval, Spanish, the time of Wallenstein, and Rococo. I do not recall seeing on the stage the beautiful dress of the Renaissance before the Meininger began to present *Othello* and the Shakespearean comedies in this period.

The principles of accuracy soon led to the finest discriminations. Duke Georg observed these variations not only by thirds of centuries as did Jakob Weiss,[81] "the father of costume history," but he also kept the characteristics of particular countries in mind.

Four plays, *Maria Stuart, Don Carlos, Egmont,* and Lindner's *The Massacre of St. Bartholomew,* which in point of time are not far apart, require entirely different costuming. In Act II of *Maria Stuart,* there is an especially interesting impression if, into the heavy, stiff splendor of the English Court, the French nobles with their attendants enter lightly and gracefully, each dressed in pale, delicate colors and in garments of a cut entirely different from that of the English. The dissimilarity of the nations —their entirely different way of life—is apparent with one stroke.

Was it the Duke's purpose to educate people by this historical accuracy? I don't believe so; he sought to know the truth for truth's sake, and the multiplicity of its forms excited his painter's eye. Actually the Meininger productions were based on scholarship; anyone who attended them gained a picture of the times in which the play was set. Is this detrimental to the poetical work? I believe I can reconcile this question, too. I am not of the opinion that Wallenstein's fate is less touching because he and his generals appear as they must have in reality. [Plate VI B] Have not our classic authors taken trouble to invest their characters with universal human traits and bestow on them real historical coloring? Who can deny

---

[80]Schiller's famous trilogy (1799) on the Thirty Years' War, 1618-48.
[81]*Cf.* p. 51.

that we can better judge a stranger if we have some information about his domestic life, his manner, his dress, etc.?

Our great poets have not set their works in vague timelessness; on the contrary, they have used time and place exactly, as a canvas for their compositions. Goethe was very earnestly concerned over the question whether the verse in *Wallenstein's Camp*, "And to Vienna the old wigs," should stand.[82] He was very pleased to find in an old book—he does not say which one—the confirmation that wigs were worn in Wallenstein's time. Incidentally, it might be remarked that if he referred to the long wig which Schiller had in mind as a symbol of pedantry, then Goethe was misinformed by the book. Wigs to disguise the lack of hair have been worn since the earliest times, but the long wig, which by no means makes any claim to pass for natural hair, came into fashion with Louis XIV.

Before the time of the Meininger, the art of costume had already approached a degree of accuracy through the influence of Paris, where painters generally had made a thorough study of historical detail in garments; but the stage costumer was still dependent upon the actor, whose taste and wishes had to be carefully taken into consideration. The becoming costume—that is, what each and everyone chose as a costume for himself— became the standard. Besides, the general point of view was that of the reviewer (perhaps Goethe) of the first performance of the *Piccolomini:* "The directors spared no expense in carrying out the sense and spirit of the play through the settings and costumes. They seem to have reached a happy medium in presenting the barbaric costumes of the time in a way pleasing to the eye "

Elaborately ornamented garments were still considered attractive in the 1860's. The men's costumes had to fit as tightly as possible and had to be embroidered on the vest; above all, they had to be open at the throat. Every gallant angrily rejected a Spanish ruff; every tenor refused it even more vehemently. It would constrain the neck and make singing and speaking difficult! It is noteworthy that such was not the case with the Meininger.

The actresses always knew how to indulge their preference for the prevailing fashion. How this happened at the time of Count von Brühl, we have already heard. Later, they managed to smuggle in the crinoline: their reaction against the narrow, close-fitting Empire gown. Photographs of Stich-Crelinger as Iphigenia at the Berlin Schauspielhaus and of Fanny Janauschek as Medea at the Meiningen Theatre show them wearing the antique draperies over many undergarments that seem almost as broad as the beloved crinoline.

Botho von Hülsen,[83] who sharply attacked the actors' arrogance and

---

[82] It was only through the encouragement of Goethe that Schiller was able to finish his *Wallenstein* trilogy. Because of his failing health, Schiller had given up his teaching post at Jena and had settled at Weimar, where he assisted Goethe in the Court Theatre.
[83] General Intendant of the Royal Playhouse in Berlin from 1851 to 1886.

presumption and who deserves respect for having restored discipline in the theatre (although sometimes he was too Prussian), possessed considerable courage to oppose the prevalent fashion. This courage should be noted because it was so rare.

On November 4, 1859, there appeared on a placard the following announcement by General Intendant von Hülsen:

> For all costumes, as well as all modern garments, absolutely without exception, the so-called crinoline is forbidden; that is to say, any undergarments which do not follow the natural movement of the body are unacceptable. The women are to make use of undergarments which allow kneeling, sitting, embracing, etc., without producing an ugly, ridiculous, or even improper appearance to the viewer in the orchestra.

I doubt very much that this proclamation spread suitable fear or had any result. Fashion pictures originating about that time seem to show the opposite to be true.

In such matters a Duke could step in with an "I wish this" or an "I order that" against which no refusal could stand. Men, as well as women, had to wear whatever was given to them. No tailor or costumer dared to change the smallest detail. This use of authority resulted in the stamp of authenticity and historical truth on both the cut of the costume and the choice of materials.

In those days, the very essence of the costumes lay in the reference to "theatre material," lighter and less expensive fabrics and velvets, which probably all came from the same company. This was usually the Katz Company in Krefeld. In almost all theatres one saw the same range of colors. These were "beautiful" colors; that is, they were extremely loud and there was a choice only between dark and light.

In Meiningen only the best and finest materials were used—weighty fabrics, fine velvet, the heaviest silks, and good furs instead of the customary rabbit. Heavy upholstery materials, woven according to old Renaissance patterns, had rarely been manufactured in Germany before the time of the Meininger. The Duke imported these materials, which were especially suited for costumes, from Genoa and Lyons. Often they were made expressly for him.

To wear Meininger robes was in the most literal sense no light task, all the more so as they were lined with a heavy fabric—I think it was called kalmuck—by which they were stiffened in order to give an appearance of greater reality.

The weapons came from Granget in Paris. Later the Duke trained in Meiningen two clever tinsmiths, Weingarten and Kallert, who prepared armor according to the Duke's sketches.

Instead of stockinet (completely sewn over with silver glitter) which was passed off as chain mail—indeed, audiences have had an opportunity to admire this sort of thing up to the most recent times in *Lohengrin*—genuine iron chain mail and armor was used in Meiningen. In addition, all iron tools were genuine. Anyone who had ever been put into the iron oven of this armor in August at Munich or Budapest under the gaslights of an already warm theatre, need look no further for a Roman steam bath. But the actor in Meiningen armor or costumes felt convincing; nothing reminded him that this was only play-acting.

The authentically styled furniture was made in Sonneberg, where wood carving is at its best. Soon there flourished in Berlin and elsewhere many companies making theatrical properties whose hundreds of workers had the Meininger to thank for their employment.

The great standard work of costume history had been begun by Jakob Weiss in 1856, but the third part did not appear until 1872. After that many excellent new works on the subject followed in quick succession. I may mention only Heyden, Kretchmar, and Hottenroth. The flourishing of this young science, too, could be placed to the credit of the Meininger.

The settings at Meiningen were also greatly admired for another reason: their design was essentially different from that usually seen in Germany, where theatre painting at that time had not attained a high standard. Although now and then worthy stage designers emerged, notably under Gropius in Berlin and Quaglio in Munich, most of those laying claim to that title had no right to it. The Schinkel school of scene design with its striving after correctness in architectural drawing and its delicate, almost insipid, use of colors was still very influential.[84] Blue and violet were the basic favorites. The laudable purpose of these designers was to create not an independent work of art, but to produce only a background. It is certainly true that the more neutral the background remains, the more vigorously the figure of the actor emerges.

The Brückner brothers of Coburg (unfortunately the younger died early) were hired by the Duke to work on the opposite principle. Brückner, who among easel painters was an outstanding landscape artist, favored as a basic tone a strong reddish-brown, the beautiful oil color known as Kassler Brown. Up to that time, the figures of the actors stood dark against a light background; now they emerged as light against a dark background.

The Duke's stage pictures can be compared with Rembrandt's paintings, whereas those of his predecessors can properly be compared to Schwind's.[85] If anyone thinks this comparison with Rembrandt too bold, let him remember the paintings of Gallait and Karl von Piloty,[86] who had influenced German painting most strongly since the 1860's. The theatre in those days did not follow painting as closely as it does today.

Undoubtedly the Duke was first stimulated in the art of scene design by the London "Revivals" of Charles Kean. Leopold Stahl has already

[84]Karl Friedrich Schinkel (1781-1841), architect and scene designer, was trained in Berlin and in Italy. He designed, among many other notable buildings, the Royal Playhouse in Berlin (1821).
[85]Moritz von Schwind (1804-71), one of the last of the German romantic painters.
[86]Louis Gallait (1810-1887), Belgian historical painter. Karl von Piloty (1826-1886), German historical painter.

commented on this in the Cologne *Zeitung,* Numbers 14 and 15, 1913. The English stage had always paid great attention to the scenic arts; as early as the eighteenth century these had reached a standard in England never approached—with a possible exception in the opera—on the primitive stages of France and Germany.

Friedrich Hasse, at that time Director of the Leipzig Municipal Theatre, imitated Kean's method of staging *Richard III, Hamlet,* and *The Merchant of Venice,* at least in the purely decorative arts. Consequently, he may be regarded as the first German forerunner of the Meininger, but between his productions and those of the Meininger a basic difference exists.

Above everything else, the former productions were designed to provide a brilliant background for the "star" and to assure for him a full house and an audience inclined to applaud; this was the goal in both London and Leipzig. The Duke, to whom nothing was more distasteful than the "star system" and solo virtuosity, based his stage designs entirely on the work of the poet.

When Paul Lindau wrote to the princely director that the principle of the Meininger was to place the poetic work in a frame worthy of it and to combine the glory with the glitter for the best effect, the Duke, on October 25, 1879, replied:

> This, my very good Sir, is certainly not the goal of my endeavors; yet I shall not deny that it is not a matter of indifference to me in what bowl golden fruit is offered. I shall also certainly not maintain that I never deceive myself about the limits to which one may go with stage decoration. Views on this point naturally are of a subjective nature, but this I can assure you, that to me the artistry or machinery is never more important than the play itself; on the contrary, a tendency to concentrate so much on externals would find in me a resolute enemy. The discussion of the question of how it happens that stage decoration plays such a great role in the reviews of the Meininger by both their friends and critics, I shall postpone until our personal meeting, to which I am looking forward with special pleasure.

CHAPTER VIII

PREPARATION FOR THE GUEST TOURS

As I have already described, the Meininger worked for years in the little town on the Werra—and in utter silence; no one suspected that here something important, even epoch-making, was maturing. Least suspecting of all were the Meininger themselves. By these I mean the inhabitants of the "Residenz," who numbered at that time about 8,000; they seldom went away from home and scarcely ever had an opportunity to compare their theatre with others. They took what was offered to them but showed they were not entirely satisfied with a program of classical productions presented over and over in rapid succession.

At first these strange new methods astonished even the actors; but the actor easily accommodates himself to every situation, and this was an unusually pleasant one.

The Duke did not approve immediately of the plan advanced by Chronegk for a guest engagement in Berlin. After all, was there not a great deal at stake? Not only would a failure cost a great deal of money, but a ruling prince also risked the danger of being made ridiculous. Chronegk proposed a plan to clear these very sensible objections out of the way. The pontiff of the Berlin critics, Karl Frenzel, was invited to visit two performances of the Court Theatre. *The Taming of the Shrew* and *Julius Caesar* were performed for him on January 1 and 2, 1870.

The Shakespearean comedy, which even later was not considered an outstanding production of the Meininger, did not make a favorable impression on the Duke's guest. He did find friendly words for the Katherine of Fräulein Ellen Franz. He also commended the concept of playing the piece in the manner of the Commedia dell'Arte; yet he believed that the actors had not wholly succeeded in carrying out this interpretation. But Frenzel was forced to express unreserved commendation for the performance of *Julius Caesar*. He also gave it a review in the literary section of the *Nationalzeitung*—somewhat cautiously, to be sure, and with a superior attitude toward the little Court Theatre. In spite of that, his article made German literary circles aware of the theatre activities in Meiningen.

After Ellen Franz became Frau von Heldburg, plans for the guest tours quickly took shape. Systematically, the season of 1873-1874 was devoted to the preparations. The plays proposed were *Julius Caesar, Twelfth Night, The Merchant of Venice,* and *The Imaginary Invalid*; from the newer works, Lindner's *The Massacre of St. Bartholomew,* Minding's *Pope Sixtus V,* and (as an afterpiece following *The Imaginary Invalid*) Björnson's *Between the Battles.* Earlier, on March 10, 1867, *Julius Caesar* had been presented with the greatest care, as can be seen from the Duke's letter on page 18 of this volume.

At this point the sets were newly painted by Brückner, using as a basis the sketches prepared by Visconti, the Curator of Ancient Monuments and Director of Archaeological Research in Rome. The Brückner sets had to be repeatedly redone. I myself recall that the background for the first act was rejected and had to be repainted.

Although no basic changes were made in the costume designs, more beautiful and more expensive materials were used in creating a new wardrobe for this production. The Duke consulted the greatest authorities in this field, and it must have been a great joy to Weiss to see on the stage togas and tunics accurately made according to his designs. The views of connoisseurs on antique costume were widely divergent, especially on the cut of the toga. In fact, it is not easy to cut the toga and drape the folds as shown on the Roman statues. Weiss had originated a special theory, which he now had an opportunity to try out.

The spirited Siegwart Friedmann describes very amusingly the experiences he had with this kind of costume when he and Ludwig Dessoir were invited as guest performers to play Cassius and Brutus on April 3, 1870:

> We had, naturally—being snobs in the provinces—brought with us our own Royal Prussian Theatre costumes and weapons. But we were notified that the Duke favored our using his costumes in order not to destroy the harmonious effect of the artistic whole. The cautious Dessoir had the Meininger costumes brought to the dressing room on the day before the dress rehearsal. What followed showed that this foresight was justified.
>
> Our Berlin togas had something of the shape of a middlesized table cover. I remember the terror with which we unfolded the Meininger monster. This genuine toga, made of real wool, measured 30 ells and weighed—I don't know how much! We first had to ask the costumer privately how, by folding and gathering it up, one should wear such a toga to make it becoming—how one should adjust it in order to be able to move at all. Since I was twenty-eight years old and slender, I soon found myself in good order; indeed, I perceived that the unusual lack of freedom which the bulk and weight of the garment imposed on me was really an advantage: my too brisk movements were hindered. My Cassius became steadier, more restrained, more Roman. I think I have never played the role better.
>
> As the gigantic ancient costume unrolled threateningly before the astonished eyes of Dessoir, he glanced perplexedly first at

the toga, then at the costumer, then at me. Finally, his wandering glance, seeking help, traversed the entire space of the dressing room, just as would that of a mourning child who has lost his way and cannot find the road home. I had to stand as a model and allow myself to be draped in order to orient him to this costume chaos. At last he seemed to understand how it was to be done; he permitted himself to be draped and made ready. But the results of our combined efforts were lamentable.

With his huge skull, his broad upper body, and his very short legs, he appeared in the bulk of the Meininger garment like a Roman nutcracker wrapped in swaddling clothes. As he surveyed himself in the mirror, he laughed out loud. I exploded, too, and even the serious costumer, who was only an employee of the theatre and had no real influence, could not keep from laughing. After a long deliberation, it was decided to cut away as much of the toga as necessary to remove the comic effect of this Brutus. He did not become beautiful, I must admit, but in a production with Dessoir one soon forgot all outward appearances and was transported by the great artistry of his performance.

Besides the technical preparation for the Berlin engagement, the question of personnel was naturally decided with great care. For Brutus, Hellmuth-Bräm was engaged; for Caesar, Joseph Nesper. Nesper, a very handsome young chap of about twenty-eight, had always played the role of the hero. Up to that time, the role of Caesar had fallen to a character actor; it was something entirely new that it was now entrusted to a leading man. In this unusual casting, the Duke reasoned that the central character of a tragedy should impress himself upon the eyes of the audience as an outwardly fine, as well as an extremely important, person. Since the role is not a large one, this argument has a certain justification; an actor who can impressively and credibly clothe it in flesh and blood is seldom found. The Meininger possessed such an actor in Josef Weilenbeck, but that artist suffered from very bad eyesight, and consideration had to be given to his progressive blindness. The assassination scene with its sudden fall down many steps would have been too difficult, a wholly impossible task for a man who had to depend on inconspicuous assistance from his co-workers. In any case, Nesper's magnificent figure carried the intended symbolic impression to its full significance.

An extremely well-characterized Cassius was portrayed by the slender, young, and intelligent character actor, Leopold Teller, of the Leipzig Municipal Theatre. The most important thing was to find a satisfactory Marc Antony who could be fitted into the already polished crowd scenes like a jewel into a costly mounting. Up to this time, the role had been given to the best speaker on the stage, one who would do justice to its spirited content. In the article previously mentioned, Karl Frenzel dedicated some very commendatory words to Weilenbeck's Antony, but in appearance the older man could not in the least measure up to the picture which one has of Caesar's worldly favorite. Especially in his first entrance when he is dressed as a runner in the Lupercalian games, in only a short black skin which left one shoulder bare, Weilenbeck made an appearance which just missed being comic.

To find a young actor who possessed the experience for this demanding role was certainly not easy. After several disappointments, success came at last: Ludwig Barnay entered the circle of the Meininger. Seldom, perhaps never, have the requirements of a role better matched the talents of an actor than in the case of this young artist with his handsome Roman head—a head also gifted and clever. [Plate VI A]

He lacked only one trait to keep us from counting him among the most outstanding exponents of his art: a profound sensitivity, a warm, genuine feeling. This quality breaks forth in the role of Antony only once, in the monologue over Caesar's bier, and Barnay was artist enough to be convincing, although not thrilling. Marc Antony's intellectual superiority, coupled with his magnificent appearance, has never been more convincingly portrayed on our stage, not even by Matkowsky[87] himself—who, in direct contrast to Barnay, based his interpretation on Antony's fervent affection for Caesar. On the other hand, in his performance the political and demagogic element was not displayed sufficiently to express the character completely.

Barnay's success in Berlin was great; he contributed much to the fame of the Meininger, but the Meininger also contributed to his. Barnay's merit in the role of Marc Antony, who can be called the determining element in the play (although, of course, Brutus is the real hero of the play) remains undiminished; but what a great part the Meininger production played in facilitating his task! Every effect which the furiously inciting speech over Caesar's bier was meant to exercise upon the mob was carefully planned and rehearsed. The gradual, attentive listening of the mob after the initial disinterest—for the warm, acceptable words of the honest Brutus continue to sound in their ears; the sudden swing to disapproval of the deed which Brutus had just finished defending successfully; the rising indignation, the emotion at the sight of Caesar's bier, the wild greediness for the will; the frightening assent, "Yes!," thundering from two hundred throats at the question, "You will compel me then to read the will?"; the rebellion; the boundless fury of the aroused crowd—all this was carefully worked out before Barnay came upon the stage for the first time. To make use of a homely expression, he needed only to lie down upon a bed already prepared for him.

But the public naturally had to think that all the emotions of the crowd were the immediate result of the orator, who therefore became doubly

---

87 Adalbert Matkowsky (1877-1909), distinguished German character actor. Grube wrote his biography, *Adalbert Matkowsky* (1909).

admired. Such co-operation between the performer and those known as "extras" was indeed something totally unknown.

In the winter of 1873 the little Berlin gentleman[88] with the Voltaire face was again seen in Meiningen, and again *Julius Caesar* was played for him. The hints which the clever critic of the *Nationalzeitung* had given in his review had obviously not been overlooked; and, indeed, he seemed more satisfied than on his first visit. At this time the resolution to make a guest appearance in Berlin was decided on conclusively. Now began rehearsal, rehearsal, rehearsal! And actually the performances were only open dress rehearsals.

The actors in Meiningen were accustomed to find many things different from those in the usual German theatre, but the incessant rehearsing and repetition of one single play, while the grumbling public was pacified with drug-on-the-market comedies, which required little time to prepare—this conduct of the management caused "much shaking of heads."

Suddenly the news of the plan for a Berlin guest engagement exploded in the midst of their monotonous work and rolled up waves of excitement. But it was a completely happy announcement only for the very young members of the company, for whom the opportunity to become thoroughly acquainted with beautiful Berlin at the Duke's expense and at double pay must have seemed very attractive. Their older, experienced colleagues expressed rather unconcealed opinions that even little princes suffer attacks of Caesar-madness and that the undertaking must certainly end in a miserable failure. In a contest with the Berlin greats, the Meininger would certainly come out on the short end. They did not realize that in this struggle much less depended on individual skills than on the power and force of the entire stage ensemble; each feared that in the inevitable defeat he would lose his own neck.

---

[88]Karl Frenzel.

CHAPTER IX

THE FIRST BERLIN GUEST ENGAGEMENT

By degrees the waves of excitement moderated, but before the curtain rose on that May 1, 1874, in the Friedrich-Wilhelm-Städtisches Theater, a surge of agitation issued from the Roman crowd in *Julius Caesar* and swept over the stage. The importance of the hour struck everyone, even though no one comprehended it clearly. Nobody remained in his place, everyone ran about, everything hummed as if in a startled beehive. Then Chronegk stepped into the middle of the stage, holding high a paper. Silence descended and everyone crowded around him. He read the telegram from the Duke, which had this droll wording:

All good luck and don't let Pfutz suffer too long.

Georg

Pfutz was a tall. skinny Voice-of-God; that is how I designated the mob players, because, as you know, the voice of the people is the voice of God. In the battle in the last act, the aforementioned Pfutz had concocted a moving death scene. The Duke was afraid that Pfutz's spasmodic death shudders would attract too much attention and perhaps evoke a result just the opposite of what Pfutz was striving for. It was the only fear tormenting the princely director at this moment which was so critical for him. If the bold venture miscarried, what a flood of caustic criticism would descend upon the head of the Theatre Duke.

The great, overwhelming sequel is well known.

Above all else, the Berliners were astonished, actually dumbfounded, by the folk scenes at the very beginning of the play. After Stoppenhagen as Casca had been applauded in the middle of the opening scene, the audience began to warm up; and if one manages to achieve that with Berliners (something not easy to accomplish), then interest usually rises to fever heat. Storms of applause broke out after the Capitol and Forum scenes and would not subside for the concluding scene.

Even earlier, the scene in Brutus' garden had evoked astonishment. This scene, as you know. is full of passionate tension. Nothing is more natural than for the actor to display here the full range of his voice; the Meininger played this scene in whispered tones. The Duke proceeded on the assumption that conspirators are not generally accustomed to cry out their plans at the top of their lungs, and in this instance the conspirators would be especially careful. Brutus' garden stands next to another's, and in the silence of night sound carries far. How easily can something discussed here fall on the ear of the eavesdropper.

It is true that this scene was inordinately difficult for the actors to perform. It is not easy to play in a large space in a whisper and still remain clear and understandable—whispering strains the voice more than speaking aloud—but it proved an effective method for expressing powerful emotions. This effect lent a sinister quality to the impressive scene. It seemed as if the enormity of the resolution oppressed every breast and strangled breath itself.

Not only was this a new interpretation; it was obvious that this was the natural, the only correct one. At this point, the audience realized that a guiding intelligence was in charge. This manner of acting the conspiracy scene has now become traditional. I do not believe it has ever again been played in the old way with the full display of voice, unless it was in that unlucky circus-type theatre[89] in Berlin, whose immense space made a whisper impossible, just as it made every fine delineation impossible.

About the performance, Karl Frenzel wrote in his *Berlin Dramaturgy:*

What marks this production of the play above all else is the avoidance of frequent scene changes. In the first act the same set is used from Caesar's entrance into the festival place up to the agreement of Cassius, Casca, and Cinna during the thunderstorm in the Roman Forum. In the second act we see the garden of Brutus and the Chamber of Caesar. Act III presents two scenes, the Curia of Pompey and the Forum with the Rostrum. In the fourth act, to my way of thinking, the first scene between the triumvirate, Octavius, Antony, and Lepidus, can be passed over as superfluous, and the whole act be played in the tent of Brutus. With great skill and artistry, the last act—the battle at Philippi— has been compressed into a single setting.

What the audience sees as scenic designs is not entirely the result of a talented painter's active imagination; everything is drawn up with a precise regard for archaeological accuracy. The view of the Roman Forum in the third act shows the Forum looking toward the Palatine; the Rostrum stands with its wider side opposite the Senate House. In the background rise the steps to the palaces and the arches of triumph. No less original and true to nature is the decor for the concluding scenes, revealing to us the battlefield of Philippi. One must imagine these unusual settings filled with heroes and heroines, with groups of people and soldiers, all of whom from head to toe give an impression of ancient Rome. Nothing of the shabby clothing that usually passes for togas, nothing of the women's headdresses with chignons in the modern style, nothing of the medieval spears and helmets usually carried by the legions! Everything, even to the head of Medusa appearing on Caesar's cloak, had an antique appearance.

---

[89] Reinhardt's Grosses Schauspielhaus.

There can be many points of view about the style of the production, but no one can deny that it moved that audience powerfully and profoundly. Not many of us have ever seen such scenes as Caesar's festive procession; his assassination; Antony's speech at the bier; the final scene, when the victors, lighted by the glow of torches, look down from a height on the "noblest Roman of them all."

The management of the masses is brought almost to perfection. When Casca stabs Caesar, the crowd around the Curia lets out a single, heart-shaking cry; then absolute silence follows. The assassins, the Senators, the masses stand for a minute as if under a spell, benumbed before the corpse of the mighty Caesar. Then a storm breaks forth, the movement of which must be seen, the roar of which must be heard, in order to realize to what height, to what power, to what profundity dramatic art can ascend. In the Forum scene other artistic and astounding moments followed, each surpassing the one before; Antony is raised on the shoulders of the crowd and in the midst of the wildest excitement reads aloud Caesar's will; the enraged populace lays hold of the bier with the corpse; others surge into the vicinity with torches; finally, Cinna, the poet, is killed in a savage tumult. One seems to be present at the beginning of a revolution.

Now we come to an adverse point of view and question the propriety of the performance: whether perhaps too much turmoil has been presented, and whether the tumult could not have been toned down a little?

Since they have the "Meininger" touch, we should mention the great battles, which in the last act moved from downstage left diagonally to up right, near the narrowed background, and then down again.

The Meininger stage battles were considerably different from those which had been presented up to that time; they were fought not with thoughtless extras, but with young actors. The battles were heated and often resulted in injuries. Although in other theatres, the crowd threshed aimlessly across the stage, here we saw soldiers really fighting with each other and realistically simulating the wounded and the dying. The setting was very restricted and the scene was staged in evening darkness—later moonlight—so that the hand-to-hand fighting seemed comparatively authentic. Nevertheless, we must approve of present-day production methods that save the time sacrificed to practicing such skills as fencing, and place the battles backstage, merely suggesting them by means of fanfares, drums, and the confused din of voices.

The appearance of Caesar's ghost produced a great sensation. This was achieved in the simplest possible way. The back of the tent was narrowed by curtains and from the passage thus produced, the apparition moved across the stage. In a dark red toga, the figure was not at first apparent against the tent wall of the same color until a beam of electric light struck its face.

Electric lighting effects were still something entirely new. The Meininger had brought on tour apparatus produced by Baer in Dresden and thereby did much to encourage the use of electricity on other stages. The means by which this ghostly figure was made to appear as if from nowhere seemed inexplicable. But how artistically was this wonder of technical skill prepared, how receptive the audience was made for it! His friends had left the tent and Brutus remained alone with his grief. Now the charming boy, Lucilius, although almost overcome by sleep, tries to cheer the grief-stricken mind of his master by playing on the harp; but while the last sad notes are floating on the air, the instrument falls from the hand of the sleeping boy. Only the disconnected words of the sorrowing man break the profound, sorrowful silence of the tent. All at once, he starts up with a sudden shriek! All this was skillfully devised and carried out.

The Meininger used the Laube version, but they played the scene of the unlucky poet, Cinna, dragged to death by the crowd; this had been omitted by Laube. This horrible-comic scene with its picture of the enraged mob made a critical impression and from that time it has been retained in all theatres. The entire last act was compressed into one setting. This showed a cut in the earth running backwards diagonally from the right, with steep walls rising on right stage. It gave the appearance of a dried-up river bed which divided the two armies and in which the conflict later took place.

The guest appearance, planned for four weeks, had to be extended fourteen days. *Julius Caesar* played twenty-two performances from May 1 to June 16—at a time when long-run performances were unknown; this was an unheard-of total.

The unusually warm attitude which the generally cool Karl Frenzel displayed and the almost unanimously enthusiastic press notices did not remain unchallenged. Paul Lindau proved himself an especially acid opponent of the Meininger. His objections were the same that today are brought against the illusionary theatre, for whose perfection the Meininger may be thanked—although one or two of their individual offerings may have been surpassed by Reinhardt or others who had at their disposal more nearly perfected scenic apparatus.

The opponents of the Meininger lived to experience the satisfaction that the company enjoyed none of the same applause for their second offering. It was clearly evident that the best and most authentic production, utilizing ensemble playing to its fullest, could not rescue a weak play. And that describes *Sixtus V* by the unfortunate Julius Minding (who, in New York, had put an end to his unsuccessful existence by his own hand).

Great hopes had been aroused by this production, which the Duke wanted to bring as an offering to the shade of the poet. August Becker, Director of the Oldenburg Court Theatre, and Klemens Raimer, the Zurich producer, had arranged the work for the stage. All was in vain. Bias had deceived literary circles about its dramatic worth. *Sixtus V* possessed only one powerful scene: after Cardinal Mentalto—who before the world has played the weak invalid—has been elevated to the Papal throne by the conclave, he throws his crutches from him and in a thundering speech reveals his true character. Weilenbeck brought his full power to this scene; yet weak action later on caused this play to fail in spite of all the splendor of the College of Cardinals with their symphony in reds, and in spite of the authenticity of the unfamiliar Roman streets of the Renaissance. *Sixtus* survived only four performances, and repeat showings of *Julius Caesar* were quickly put on the boards.

But this stain was completely obliterated. With the opening of *Twelfth Night* the Meininger won a new triumph, all the greater because the Royal Playhouse had achieved a great success with the comedy the previous winter. In this instance, even the bitterest enemies of the Meininger could not be critical about confusion in mass scenes or about splendor and over-decoration that distracted from the play. This production of the Shake-spearean comedy was given in a manner more simplified than anyone had ever seen before.

For this play the Meininger created a pattern which many theatres have since used with very little variation. With the exception of two small rooms, put up quickly within the setting, the scene did not change during the whole performance. On the left stood Olivia's house with a set of steps, over which honeysuckle twined, leading to the second floor. Somewhat farther to the right in the background was a less prominent building, so that one seemed to find himself in a park, intersected by a public road. Nowadays, both room settings are usually omitted—a lack which in fact is not too great an assault on the play. Probably no present-day director knows that this simplification of the setting originated with the Meininger.

The expressionistic[90] theatre of today renounces every indication of reality and places the play in an architectural frame, and from an expressionistic point of view, there can be no objection to this.

Shakespeare set his play in Illyria—as we would say, in a romantic land—in which imaginative "timeless" costumes could be used. The Meininger used those of the Elizabethan period. This play is often presented in the artistic costumes of the fifteenth century, adding to its lyrical-poetical qualities; but for the humorous scenes the appeal of "merrie old England" seems definitely more fitting. The riotous behavior of Sir Toby and the foppish dress of the aristocratic Christoph[91] is better set forth as English; moreover, the drinking bout is not especially characteristic of Southern Europe.

---

[90]Defined by Grube in his Preface.
[91]Sir Andrew Aguecheek is called Christoph von Bleichenwang in the German version.

We have the Meininger to thank also for discarding the Deinhardstein textual revision, which up to that time had dominated all German productions. This monstrous stupidity made of Viola, Cesario, and Sebastian a starring role for a clever actress. For a really skillful actress, of course, this was very effective; if she understood how to assume a deeper speaking voice and vary her movements, it was not hard. Directors were spared the trouble of seeking a brother and sister who are almost identical in appearance.

The Meininger had the good fortune to possess in Klara Hausmann and Franz Wallner suitable performers; that is, the handsome young Wallner was engaged especially for the part. The showy costume sketched by the Duke did its duty in the mistaken identity scenes, which were played by moonlight, as was the whole last act. In the last act—in which both characters appear at the same time—one or the other continually turned his back to the audience without appearing to do so artificially.

Another innovation introduced by the Meininger has since been adopted in all productions. The song "Come Away, Come Away, Death," was sung, not by the Fool, but by Viola. Shakespeare purists may shake their heads over that, but the effect of the song is heightened by this device. It really suits the character of Viola, who has entered the service of the Duke as a singer.

It was very useful to the Meininger to have a setting that surpassed that of the Berliners, something I can attest from my own observation. It must be admitted that the Meininger actor could not approach the incomparable Malvolio of Döring, and it was a great success for him that he could sneak through with a whole skin.

Klara Hausmann, a gay and spirited person, was perfectly suited for the poetic qualities as well as the humor of Viola. One of the best Marias I have ever seen was Fanny Weidt. She would have had a distinguished career in the theatre, had she not been enticed away by a Frankfurt merchant. It is by no means easy to describe what an elf lay in that tiny, delicate figure.

On one occasion she was the reason for the inclusion by the Meininger of a scene just for her. She was seen above on the steps about to report that Malvolio was falling into the trap of the forged letter. At the first general rehearsal she entered laughing, and she continued to laugh until she could not remember her first words; this brought Sir Toby and Fabian also to laughter. With a genial glance the Duke caught up the accidental incident, and the scene was directed in the following manner:

Maria is seen above. Full of her breezy news, she begins to laugh; Toby and Fabian come to the foot of the stairs and ask her in pantomime the reason for this great merriment. Maria tries to speak, but she cannot speak for laughing; twice, three times, she begins, but always in vain. This seems extremely funny to those standing below and, little by little, they begin to laugh. Laughing, as we all know, is as catching as yawning. When

Maria has descended the steps, bent over from laughing, she must sit on a step, and then Toby and Fabian break into resounding laughter.

This bubbling gaiety with no visible reason, pricking our curiosity to learn what lay behind it, had something so overwhelmingly funny that the artists were always rewarded after this wordless laughing bout with a round of applause.

Little by little, Maria recovers herself enough so that she can relate the facts about the yellow stockings and the other follies of the humbugged steward. With the main catchwords of the report, she is interrupted by gales of laughter which increase more and more until the merry trio, holding each other up and weaving from laughter, disappear from the scene.

The audience always thanked them with loud applause, but to make the scene a success the actors must be able to offer laughter as silvery fresh as could little Fanny Weidt and as heartwarming as that of Hellmuth as Toby.

Whenever I have staged *Twelfth Night,* I always modeled this scene on the Meininger pattern, and it never lacked success. Much laughter has become traditional in this play; but without the arrangements, the divisions, and the gradations that were discovered after long rehearsals in the Meininger production, the scene degenerates into confusion.

The Duke, as well as Chronegk, approached his problems in a completely unprejudiced way. An old stage expert would never have risked such a laughing scene, for it is a proved rule of the stage that the actor who wishes to make others laugh must never do so himself. That is true in general, but here the rule is proved by a splendid exception.

I have seen many excellent Marias: Paula Conrad, Berta Hausner, Fräulein Gasny, Fräulein Wangel, but never again a Sir Toby like that of Hellmuth-Bräm. The role cannot "be murdered," as the actor says; it would be almost impossible not to produce a success with it. But very often on our stages the merry nobleman, rising wittily above his surroundings, becomes a fat drunkard, a beer—not a wine—consumer. Hellmuth's merriment in his cups was clothed in a grand manner and courtly deportment, indescribably droll and at the same time, I must say, winning, so that the hearty figure became sympathetic.

Teller made a clever, nimble fool; and Chronegk was no poor Aguecheek, although he was not as effective in this type of role as when he played a falsetto-speaking simpleton. In the continuous-state-of-drunkeness of the role, he lacked that modest alcoholic stupor with which, for example, Artur Vollmer and Hugo Thimig knew how to elevate this figure into a very special atmosphere.

After this battle was won, triumph followed triumph.

The young dramatist, Paul Lindner, had attracted attention in 1866, when he received the second Schiller Prize for *Brutus and Collatinus*—

although its performance did not confirm the decision of the judges. Three other tragedies were never performed, so far as I know, but he proved himself extraordinarily able as a dramatist with his *Massacre of St. Bartholomew*. The reception of this play, hot-tempered and fairly breathing of the struggle between state and church, was excellent (although, to be sure, he hacks away at the theme with a wood-axe).

This production was grist for the mill of those who opposed the Meininger, for, in the opinion of that time, the splendid setting was really too elaborate. Laid in the court of Charles IX, it offered the strange costumes of the French dandies. These aroused curiosity, and what didn't the audience get to hear![92]

Now, for the first time, the Meininger displayed their ability to organize and orchestrate commotion behind the scenes and to make it serviceable in producing a unified effect—something which up to that time had not been given much notice. The ringing of the bells on St. Bartholomew's night, the victorious song of the Huguenots breaking forth: "A Mighty Fortress Is Our God," while nearby gay dance music rings out from the rooms of the Louvre—this chaos of sound was thrilling. The imagination painted all the terrors of the frightful night, and yet, for all that, the performance was not drowned out or stifled. These effects received their full and justly fair share of the praise for the production.

Next to Barnay's interesting Henry of Navarre, Frau Berg's[93] characteristically fine Catherine de Medici, and Frau von Moser-Sperner's passionate Marguerite de Valois, stood Leopold Teller as a first rate Charles IX. This decadent character, wavering between goodness and evil, between justice and ambition, suited this artist especially well; it was the case of a role "written for an actor."

Following this, the Berliners again were offered "Rrr, another picture,"[94] again a play without highly decorated sets and splendid costumes, and without an emphasis on "masses": Molière's *The Imaginary Invalid*. Here it would be best for me to quote from the words of Karl Frenzel, for by now my praise might be somewhat suspect:

> The production of Molière's *The Imaginary Invalid* has refuted the objection—if any proof is needed for the unprejudiced—that scenery is the basis of the Meininger's success. Here was very little scenery: a room with a sort of alcove in which stands Argan's bed, a table with medicine bottles, and a few armchairs. In this space our guests carried off Molière's comedy with truth, gaiety, freshness, and humor, so that for an hour and a half the audience never stopped laughing. The charm of the Meininger presentations lies in their harmonious development and in the fact that they lend body and spirit to the play. Thus in *Julius*

92"Was gab es hier nicht auch zu hören!"
93Marie Berg (d. 1890), one of the first members of the Meininger.
94"Rrr, ein ander Bild."

Caesar they bring to everyone who possesses an historical point of view the revolutionary element; in *Twelfth Night,* the moonlight, the music, and the intoxication; in the *Massacre of St. Bartholomew,* the gloomy imagination, dissolute sensuality, and melodrama; and in the same way in Molière's comedy they give an entirely unique personification to the mockery of the doctors and to the ridiculous yet intrinsically tragic qualities of this play about sickness and death. Of all the performances on the tour this was the most nearly perfect.

So far as I know the German stage, I have never seen anyone remotely approach the performances of Herr Weilenbeck as Argan [Plate VII A] and Fräulein Weidt as Toinette. Herr Weilenbeck provided his Argan with an abundance of the drollest characteristics: his first monologue; the quarrel scene with Toinette; the frolic with little Louis; his awakening from pretended death as his wife tries to steal the strongbox with the gold; the smile, in spite of his closeness to death, which passes over his face as his weeping daughter throws herself at his feet. What truth! What humor is here! The constant interchange between real and fancied illness produces the most delightful results. A happy breeze blows through this production; from the first words of the actors, the audience is in sympathy with them. Fräulein Weidt's Toinette is that handmaiden of the poet to whom he is said to have read his comedy aloud: so dainty and so roguish, so fresh and so humorous, she softens her rudeness by her laughter and her delightfulness, revealing through every trait her naturalness and sunny charm. In the interlude between Acts I and II—the curtain does not fall—she has nothing to do except to put the bed and room in order, and that pantomime alone brought her the most enthusiastic applause. Even supercilious onlookers, who at first had turned up their noses, had at last to laugh with the others.

The straightening of the bed was not written in by Molière; it was a stage direction of the Duke, who did not want to lower the front curtain. He did not favor the traditional three raps which, in France, indicate the intermission. In order to continue the play there was a pillow fight, which grew out of tossing a pillow back and forth between Argan and Toinette. This, too, had not been suggested by the poet. The pillows were still lying around the set, and this merry solution answered the question of how they were to be removed. The break between the second and third acts was indicated by having a servant carry a large incense burner to all parts of the room. That seemed as characteristic as it was amusing.

I must mention a few examples of Weilenbeck's acting that were equally amusing, and by this I hope to earn a special "thank you" from other Argans and other directors of *The Imaginary Invalid.* He differentiated very carefully between the two exits which he had to make in haste during the course of the play.

"Come nearer, Angelique," he said the first time. "I should like to communicate something to you." He spoke this lovingly, with honest, fatherly tenderness. Abruptly, some pressing motive took him from the room. Shortly thereafter, he returned in a better humor. The affair for which he had withdrawn had succeeded exactly as he had wished. Then the following scene demanded that he display a happy disposition above all else.

But when he returns from a similarly sudden and urgent disappearance in the third act, he is very dissatisfied. Consequently the next scene begins in a growling tone—and with good reason. The role abounds with such nice points, and not a single one seemed a pure bid to tickle a laugh from the audience. Each was integrated with the role and the play.

Later Molière demands that the actor of the title role again repeat an action: awakening from pretended death to test both his wife and his daughter on the sincerity of their sentiments. Madame Beline, as we know, made a poor showing on this test. It was very amusing to see how the face of the seemingly dead Argan revealed itself as pained or angry whenever he fancied himself unobserved and then sank quickly back into a state of death. It had a tremendously comical effect when Argan, as his wife bent over him to take the key from his pocket, lifted his arm slowly and allowed his hand to hover over her head like an avenging Nemesis and then let it drop with a sudden grasp. When the unmasked wife ran horrified from the room with a terrible shriek, he sprang up, threw a blanket about his body as a toga and, the mighty triumphant victor, strutted up and down with proud steps. But when the gentle Angelique sank down weeping at his chair, he gave an entirely different sign of life—quickly he lifted one leg upright into the air.

Weilenbeck was an Austrian and that might very well be the reason why he put into this role something of the "Thaddädel"[95] of the old Vienna folk-plays. To be sure, it is difficult to explain exactly wherein the comedy lay—but who can really describe the art of comedy? It was a childlike and childish action, but it was also the artlessness of a grown man who is enjoying his own joke. Weilenbeck certainly never sank to a mere buffoon.With all this fun he remained a truly funny, yet always real man, and through all the "Thaddädel" characteristics his deliberately roguish spirit sparkled.

No one who saw this jolly man give his wit and humor full play, no one who had to laugh over his nimble agility when he chased the impudent maid Toinette around the table at full speed, could surmise that he was watching a blind man. By degrees, Weilenbeck had become totally blind.

---

[95] Thaddädel was the middle-aged comic character created by the actor Anton Hasenhut (d. 1841) in the Viennese folk theatre. The Thaddädel character was impetuous, childish, clumsy, and spoke with a soprano voice. Hasenhut was noted for his "skillful clumsiness." Hanswurst in the German folk play was a somewhat comparable character, and both are probably related to the Commedia dell'Arte.

It bordered on the unbelievable that he could find his way around on the stage in the midst of tables and chairs closely placed together, all the time computing distances by counting steps. Of course, his co-workers must have given him untold help, yet what an enormous willpower he must have had to overcome blindness to such a degree. Because of this he was not a little proud, but who can blame him?

"I am the first and only blind actor," he was accustomed to say. Luckily, he never learned that he had a predecessor in the eighteenth century, the manager, Nachtigall, about whom the Berlin *Literatur und Theater Zeitung* of 1781 wrote—without, however, making much ado about the fact of his blindness. Nachtigall was a Hanswurst of the improvised comedies. He must, therefore, have possessed willpower and spirit similar to that of Weilenbeck.

As a curtain raiser for the Molière play, the Duke again decided to undertake the experiment of producing a play by an author practically unknown in Germany. Björnson's *Between the Battles*[96] was then put on the boards for the first time. For the first piece of the evening, this one-act play—which glorified the twelfth century King Sverre, fighter for a unified Norway—was a good choice. Before the lightness and grace of Molière, the weight, the heavy, slow-moving tempo! The roughly framed, beamed hut, the floor covered with fir twigs, the clumsy leather and fur clothing— all this formed the greatest possible contrast to the following play, which then seemed like a brighter beam of light, like liberation from the gloomy, misty world of the north.

Björnson's play interested, yet it seemed too strange. A public not yet accustomed to exploring subject matter from such remote areas would not accept it.

On June 15 and 16, 1874 the engagement closed with *The Merchant of Venice*. In spite of a production that featured authentic Venetian backgrounds and the notable performance of Weilenbeck as Shylock, the play did not achieve a success as great as its predecessors. The weather had already become very warm, and the public was probably getting tired. We must also confess that this performance was still not as thoroughly worked out or as balanced as it was in a later production in 1886.

With the guest engagement crowned in glory, the Meiningen Court Theatre vanished from sight, so to speak, and in its place stepped the "Meininger." What a reputation the name of this previously ignored little town on the Werra had won for itself was revealed in the fall of 1874 when a fire reduced it to a third of its size. From all over Germany flowed the most generous contributions for the place whose name was in the mouth of everyone.

96Björnstjerne Björnson (1832-1910), friend, benefactor, and rival of his greater country-man, Ibsen. This was his first play (1857).

CHAPTER X

THE SECOND BERLIN ENGAGEMENT

Not in the least dazzled by their newly won triumph, the artistic trio responsible for the Meininger began in the fall with all the old earnestness and fervor to prepare for a second Berlin guest engagement, which this time was arranged for two months, April 16 to June 15, 1875.

The two plays selected as the core for this engagement were *The Battle of Arminius*[97] and *Fiesko*.[98]

Kleist's drama had already been produced during that winter at the Royal Theatre in Berlin. Was this by chance? Or was it by design? In Meiningen it was generally believed to be the latter, and not without some foundation. It was easy to believe that the Royal Theatre wanted to "steal the thunder" of the Meininger. Herr von Hülsen [99] was not their friend, for the Meininger had given the press, never favorably inclined toward the Royal Theatre, an opportunity to make some rather disagreeable comparisons. It is a fact, often confirmed, that in the theatre a first impression is the lasting one, especially if a play—as was here the case—had never been seen before on the Berlin stage. In any case, the Meininger production would lack the great charm of novelty.

The Royal Theatre production was splendidly received and was repeated many times. Not without apprehension did the troops of the Duke enter the arena this time. Yet their Field General was justified in calmly watching them march forward. His son, Prince Ernst, who later developed into an excellent painter, had been staying for a time in the capital and had reported to his father in detailed letters concerning the production at the Royal Theatre. These letters were embellished with all sorts of delightful illustrations, which the Duke later showed me.

At the Royal Theatre there were certain older actors, very well suited to second-rank middle-class plays and comedies, who did not cut handsome figures in a costume play. It was taken as a matter of course in Meiningen

---

97*Hermansschlacht* was written during the Napoleonic Wars by Heinrich von Kleist (1771-1811). It concerns itself with the historic defeat of the Romans under Varus by the Germans under Hermann (called Arminius by the Romans) in A.D. 9. The Romans were pushing east to the Elbe when Hermann, who had been a Roman citizen and soldier, secretly gathered a great force of allies and attacked Varus in the Teutoberg Forest. The Romans were totally defeated and never again made a serious attempt to annex territory east of the Rhine. The secondary plot concerns Thusnelda and her revenge on an unfaithful Roman lover, whom she causes to be crushed by a bear.

98One of Schiller's earliest plays (1783).

99General-Intendant of the Royal Theatre. Grube earlier mentions his attempts at costume reform.

that the greatest importance should be placed on the pleasing and distinguished stage presence of the actors. A knight as fat as the jolly portrayer of Korb in the *Journalists* would not have been allowed to appear in a classical production in Meiningen.

Moreover, secondary players from the opera had to be employed in the large Berlin productions. A really hefty basso once created a theatre anecdote as Titinius in *Caesar,* when he spoke every word like a deep *"Doch"* (famous to opera lovers in *The Magic Flute*):
"I ... will ... be ... here ... a ... gain ... e ... ven ... with ... a ... thought ... ," and then slowly and solemnly left the stage.

The Meininger would never have attempted anything with a director under whom such things were possible.

I have already made comparisons between the Berlin and Meininger productions in my *Youthful Recollections,* and since I cannot pass them over here, I must beg permission to quote myself:

> I had hardly arrived in Berlin when, needless to say, I hurried to *The Battle of Arminius.* Far more certain of victory than in the previous year, I was counting on its complete success.
>
> Splendor was emphasized above everything else, and it seemed as if this was exactly what the poet had wanted. For Kleist had written at the beginning of Act III, scene 6: "The Roman army passes in full splendor."
>
> At first sight the entrance of the Roman army into the Teutoberg Forest might appear as a purely decorative touch to a scene that could progress just as well if the army marched behind the scenes, and only martial music were heard. Theatres which do not have at their disposal the necessary means of handling such a scene—and our present day stylists and theatre iconoclasts who simply cut out everything which appears to be superfluous in scenic decorations—would probably have done it that way. But Kleist had conceived the Roman march, not as a scenic addition, but as an integral part of the play. Rome's entire might, against which Hermann has to fight, must be evident to the eyes of the audience at once; only then her total annihilation in the following battle scenes—which on the stage naturally are shown only in small incidents—can be fully realized. If the staging was to fulfill the intentions of the poet, it had to create the impression of an overwhelmingly massed army.
>
> How did the Meininger achieve this?
>
> First of all, in the way they narrowed the acting area as much as possible. Duke Georg had noticed that on the stage it is easier to counterfeit a large number of men if they move in a smaller space, just as a monument looks mightier if the place in which it stands is small. Reinhold Begas was accustomed to attribute the

impressive appearance of the Colleoni essentially to the location of that masterly work. And who would deny that even the colossus of Schilling's "Germania"[100] is lost in the wide expanse of landscape.

The setting represented a square in a German town. [Plate VII B] Huge beamed fences enclosed the houses; a great mound, shaded by the mighty linden sacred to the Germans, rose on the left; next to this a narrow path led to the settlement. Through this path, in which at the most four men could march abreast, the marching columns of Roman soldiers squeezed, pressed, and pushed, while the mound and the forebuildings were thickly covered with the watching German folk.

In simple, dark grey armor and helmets of iron, with packs hanging from their javelins, the troops entered, naturally not in military step. [Plate VIII A] An especially happy directorial touch was this: the army flowed through that narrow lane obliquely from downstage up to the background, so that the audience saw no faces, only helmets and armor-plated backs, as if an iron stream pressed, surged, and flooded its way toward the Teutoberg.

At the Royal Theatre the picture presented had been entirely different. The stage was very deep and seemed even more so, because the backdrop was painted to portray a valley in which separate huts appeared.

There was no break whatever in the wide stage space; it formed a huge rectangle bounded by forest wings. Over this great, open space came the Roman army marching with resounding steps. It was a magnificent army; many of the campaigners were very handsomely dressed in shining helmets and armor. In rank and file they moved with a correct Prussian goose-step directly across the stage from right to left parallel to the footlights. No one could doubt that the alert Prussian National Guard, garbed in Roman equipment, was making a formal parade across the stage.

Their acting, too, was not outstanding. Maximilian Ludwig, whose superior capabilities lay in another sphere, could not physically depict the triumphant hero, whereas Nesper,[101] aided by his extremely powerful and youthfully handsome appearance, succeeded. Berndal's Marbod was the only truly distinguished performance in Berlin, but the Marbod of Hellmuth-Bräm was also worth seeing.

The Meininger *Battle of Arminius* received enthusiastic applause and perhaps contributed to the end of the old traditional

---

100Verrocchio's equestrian statue of Bartolomeo Colleoni is in a small square in Venice. Johannes Schilling's monumental "Germania" (1883) stands in the Niederwald.

101Josef Nesper remained in the Meininger company from 1874 to 1884. He was especially successful as Fiesko.

ways of staging as they were exhibited in the Berlin production, and helped to prepare the way for newer methods. Since the comparison was obvious, it was easily drawn.

Still one more thing should be brought out to demonstrate what differentiated the Meininger presentation from that of the Berlin theatre.

Whereas Marbod's tent in the latter displayed the usual painted draperies, the Meininger set showed rough skins sewn together, which stretched around a mighty oak. A set painted with extreme skill provided a splendidly characteristic frame for the Suevi chief. The Berlin painter had pictured the Teutoberg Forest in a fitting manner with powerful tree trunks, but the ground on which these stood was level; it was plainly the stage floor. In the Meininger setting a giant fallen tree obstructed the narrow path, which the underbrush and bushes still left somewhat free. [Plate VIII B] Varus and the Roman leaders were obliged to clear a pathway with great difficulty and to climb over the trunk. It was obvious that an unexpected attack in this wild, marshy, matted forest would be crushing. How much greater the purely picturesque effect was need be mentioned only incidentally.

In costuming, too, the Meininger were more richly outfitted than the Berliners; even the German barbarians were not denied a certain elegance.

As had been the case with the presentation of *Caesar,* the princely couple had carefully noted Frenzel's observations in his review of the Royal Theatre production of *The Battle of Arminius.* On the whole, they paid the greatest attention to all reviews. Frenzel had not felt that the very large actress playing Alraune should thunder her mysterious words against the Roman General. He also made some pertinent observations about the lighting in the Alraune scene. The Meininger witch was a little, old, bent-over woman, dressed in rags. She carried a faintly glowing pine torch in her hand, and her thrice repeated, "Nevermore," hissed like a snake.

The text used was almost the same as the one employed at the Royal Theatre, that of Rudolf Genée, who merits our thanks for reawakening the great song of hate.[102] At this time a strong pressure was developing to drop revisions and elaborations in various scripts in order to restore original works for use on the stage. Genée had cut a certain terrible scene, bordering on the unendurable, in which Thusnelda turns the unsuspecting Ventidius—who believes himself about to start on another love adventure—over to the murderous "she-bear" of Cheruska. This cut was usually considered fortunate, yet the Meininger retained the scene. An historically true production permitted no comic element to be introduced and the appearance of the bear might very easily do just that. In a narrowed set,

---

[102]Grube calls *The Battle of Arminius* a "song of hate," for that is what Kleist meant it to be—a play embodying his hatred for the French. Varus and the Roman Army are symbolically Napoleon and the French army, which invaded Germany just eighteen hundred years after the Romans.

enclosed by great boulders, the monster in clanking chains could hardly be seen as it was led under the darkness of night to its prison. The impression made by this dreadful scene justified its inclusion.

Genée had also considered it necessary to omit the scene in which Hermann and Fust struggle for the honor of cutting down the enemy. This scene, too, unforgettable in its barbaric nobility, was retained by the Meininger; but some lines added by Genée to strengthen the end of the play were rightly blue-penciled.

After Kleist's great patriotic play had been performed twelve times, there followed a cheerful reversal: Molière's *The Learned Ladies*. Grillparzer's charming *Esther* fragment preceded this short play; needless to say, the production of *Esther* omitted the last scene, a change by which the play was given at least a satisfactory ending.[103] If I am not mistaken, it was the first production of Grillparzer's poetic work, one more attempt to pave the way for a play yet unknown. This time it proved successful, and a new precious jewel was set into the diadem of the German theatre. Splendid stage pictures strengthened the presentation; even the Brückner background was greeted with applause. Nesper, with his exceedingly fine figure, made a brilliant appearance in the authentically designed old Assyrian costumes. Frau von Moser-Sperner, an actress of unbelievable versatility, was a sensitive Esther. In the repeat performance, the role was entrusted to the young beginner, Hedwig Dohm, daughter of Ernst Dohm.[104] Her charming tone, her fine oriental beauty, and her wonderful eyes contributed to the success with which she passed this test. She later forsook her career, which had begun so successfully, for a marriage to a well-known scholar.

The Learned Ladies was "as good as new," at least for Berliners. If not so overwhelmingly funny as *The Imaginary Invalid,* this comedy produced great merriment through superior co-operation of the performers. But, unfortunately, the German stage could not be won over in spite of the masterly translation of Ludwig Fulda. Apparently the German understanding of Molière could not progress beyond *Tartuffe, The Imaginary Invalid,* and *The Miser.*

Weilenbeck's humorous Argan was seen five times this year. Since *Between the Battles* did not please the public even this time, the successful *Esther* took its place.

The high point of the engagement was *Fiesko*. [Plate IX B] Weakest of all Schiller's dramas, this play had never enjoyed great favor. The unusual, stilted speech was not pleasing, but, more important, the mixture

---

103Grillparzer completed only the first two acts of *Esther*. He probably abandoned the play fearful of religious and political censorship. Perhaps no other work by Grillparzer has evoked such unanimous praise from twentieth-century critics.
104Dramatist and adapter for various Berlin theatres.

of lion and fox which the poet tried to combine in the character of the hero seems incredible to honest Germans.[105] If on this occasion the work commanded twenty-two performances, then it must be admitted that the singularly splendid production added much to it. A play so seldom seen on the stage carried a certain charm of novelty, and at the Berlin "Royal" Theatre such a "republican" tragedy was certainly not often offered.

I have mentioned the splendid production, but it by no means surpassed the standard which, after the Meininger school had prevailed, was required and established by every first-rate theatre. I later worked in a much more dazzling production at the Dresden Court Theatre, which was one of the first to adopt the new methods. In 1875, however, people were still astonished by what was later accepted as matter of course. The Meininger abandoned Schiller's stage instructions: "The costume of the nobility is entirely black," for this mode did not predominate until long after Fiesko's death, when it was introduced from the gloomy Spain of Philip II. The costuming showed the gay colors of the fifteenth century; velvets, silks, and costly brocades proclaimed the wealth of proud Genoa, and made it seem comprehensible that to steal the ducal crown of such a city would be "god-like."

In this production the first act was especially striking. In place of the prescribed hall, a courtyard with orange trees was shown in Fiesko's castle. Of course, this made it impossible for Fiesko to notice in the mirror the suspicious movements of the Moor, as Schiller directs. On the other hand, the courtyard lying in the moonlight, flanked by two staircases; the lighted windows; and the reddish glow coming from the open portal—all these made a pleasing appearance. Since the business of the mirror was dropped, a very good effect was achieved when the head of the black man suddenly appeared on the highest balcony, disappeared, and then reappeared, as the sinister guest, like a feline animal of prey, began little by little to creep down the steps.

It made an especially fine picture when the group of departing guests reached the high steps on either side just as Gianettino flung his glass from above into the courtyard with a crash.

Fiesko's chamber was extraordinarily fine—black with gold fittings. When he wished "to relax in the open," he drew aside the heavy velvet curtain from the great middle arch, and through the dark frame appeared "his majestic city," radiant in the brightness of the morning sun. One must always remember how powerful the mysterious charm of electric lighting must have been in the time of gas lights, a charm to which we have become today completely indifferent. The Meininger were clever enough to use this effect very sparingly.

---

[105] In *Fiesko* Schiller used as the basis of the plot a conspiracy in sixteenth century Genoa. Fiesko becomes involved in overthrowing the honest but elderly Duke Andreas, who has allowed his powers to be usurped by his nephew, Gianettino, and his niece, Julia. Beginning as a sincere republican, Fiesko becomes consumed by a desire for power, seizes the throne, and is finally drowned by an old man, Verrina. Duke Andreas is restored to the throne, but only after the tragic death of Fiesko's lovely wife, Leonore, whom Fiesko has mistaken for his prime enemy.

A masterpiece of realistic art characterized the last act. Today the director would simply place the storming of St. Thomas' Gate behind the scenes; in those days he felt obliged to place on the stage everything the poet called for. It is possible to ridicule this point of view now, but then it was standard procedure; and it explains the success of the Meininger—that incredible march of victory—when we realize that they fully embodied the artistic views of their day and that they did it in an entirely natural way. The Duke never held the view that he should dumbfound an audience by something completely unheard of; to him his productions seemed the simplest and the most natural in the world.

The peculiarity of the last act was that it was set in the interior of St. Thomas' Gate, a fort commanding the harbor. [Plate IX A] In the moonlight lay a rather small square, enclosed by high buildings. A large fountain occupied a part of the right side; left and right ran two narrow streets; a huge gate extended diagonally across the stage from right to left. The gate itself was not in moonlight, and the whole back wall lay in deep shadows. According to the poet's instructions, a few men with lanterns cross the square. Then in a moment, while the square is nearly empty, two figures quickly approach each other, whisper something, and rapidly disappear as the guard returns. Some of the foot soldiers cross to the guard house by the gate; others stretch out on the steps of the fountain.

Again silence!

Then the distant buzzing of the crowd arises; the bells begin to herald an assault; nearer and nearer presses the uproar; the soldiers have sprung up, seizing their weapons; their comrades tumble out of the guard room. Resounding blows are struck against the gate from the outside. The iron-studded crossbars withstand the axe blows of the insurgents, but separate planks in the wooden gate are broken out. Through these gaps the troops of the revolutionists can be seen; the bright moonlight glitters on their weapons. At the open places in the gate struggles ensue. The rebels seem to be forced to retire, then—an explosion! A bomb blasts the whole gate apart; the insurgents press in, and, after a short struggle, put the defenders to flight. The confused crowd forces its way through the street on the right, next to the gate. Now the stage is left free for the next scene, which follows with breathtaking haste.

The advantages of playing the scene in this manner are evident. In addition to the picturesqueness achieved by the contrast between the few spots of light visible behind the dark gate at the beginning with the whole harbor gleaming in the moonlight and framed by the black arches of the wall after the explosion, there was also the effect of the surging masses moving from the back of the stage to the front. On the stage that movement, as is well known, gives an entirely different impression of power and might than would have been the case had the scene been set outside the fort. Then the fort would have had to be placed at the back in order to give a free view of the harbor, and the crowd would have had to surge away from the audience rather than toward it.

A fine subtlety characterized the fourth act. Andreas has appeared, surrounded by his German body guard. As he sinks down by the body of his nephew, Calagno emerges from the background with the conspirators. Their swords are gleaming, and around the left arm of each is rolled a Spanish cloak—such as would be used as the substitute for a shield—but the Italians evidently do not trust themselves to approach too close to the Germans. When the Italians finally begin the assault, they are soon forced to withdraw from Andreas and flee. The foot soldiers, however, do not leave at once; they wait to see if another attack will follow. When it seems that "respect for the Greybeard" has been whipped into the "Italian dogs," the bravely loyal Germans break into loud laughter and, taking Duke Andreas in their midst, shoulder arms and march calmly off.

This scrap of humor, brought into the frightful events of the night, lighted the scene just as does a little sunshine in a thunderstorm. Now some pious Friars cross the square, seeking the wounded and the dead. They stumble upon Gianettino's corpse and carry it away. Thus this incident, too, was made to look perfectly natural. It seemed just as believable that Fiesko could mistake his wife for the arch enemy of Genoa because of Gianettino's red cloak—in which Leonore had wrapped herself. Leonore, of course, had not entered alone; she was swept along by the disorderly crowd, which whirled across the stage. From this surging crowd the scarlet cloak and the yellow plume of the skull cap were clearly evident. Fiesko pressed forward into the crowd and lunged at her blindly.

"Through the forced gate," says Bulthaupt of the scene, "the nearly empty galley, which Fiesko is supposed to visit, is not visible lying unrealistically close to the beach; instead we see a gondola with a boatman. It is the gondola from which Verrina with his daughter and son-in-law have just landed and into which the two lovers later climb to row to the galley. While boarding the gondola, Verrina pushes the Duke into the water. The astonished boatman greets this unexpected and terrible event with every evidence of fright until, having in vain tried to rescue the Duke, he rows off to seek aid. All this is possible as can be, if one wishes to remain true to Schiller."

I must confess that I cannot agree with this praise by Bulthaupt. I find the scene very awkwardly conceived. In the first place, if we consider only what is probable, in many harbors quite large ships lie close to the quay, and a plank leads to them. That the galley is empty is quite easily explained: the crew is away because of the uprising, while the galley slaves to whom the new Duke is to announce their deliverance languish, chained in the interior of the ship. The little boat that is to carry the characters to the unseen warship in the Meininger production seems really diminutive; and the boatman, a silent witness, appears like an obtrusive, trivial figure in a painting which should portray only two great figures standing against each other, man to man, observed by no one. However good the silent pantomime is, to me at least it seems unnatural that a man present at such an incident should not break into a cry—especially an Italian.

No, here the Meininger made a virtue of necessity—if a virtue it was. Since the galley, even if it were constructed on an impossibly small scale, would have overwhelmed the entire set on the comparatively small stage, they hit upon the expedient described above.

In the text they had followed Schiller faithfully with only a few cuts of really bombastic passages. Not until the last act did they introduce any variations. The scene in which Fiesko rings the house bell to warn Andreas Doria was dropped. The scene is certainly naive, as are many situations in this youthful work. But the scene does in some measure tip the scales in favor of the hero's character, and he certainly does need that. The Duke of Saxe-Meiningen could not get over the fact that the Duke of Genoa should be seen as a porter, ringing a bell; it also seemed wrong to him that the Doge's palace lay next to St. Thomas' Gate.

It is in these scenes that one can perceive the superiority of the modern art of staging over that of the Meininger. The characteristic qualities of the two leading individuals in the play were neglected out of consideration for the scenic effects. On the other hand, it was certainly reasonable that Berta did not come on the stage disguised as a boy; in that respect the Meininger went back to the text as amended by Schiller for the Leipzig Theatre. Berta's monologue was cut, and the scene was not played in a "subterranean vault." Burgognino entered with the freed Berta from behind the gate. The boat on which Verrina had appeared then carried away the lovers "to Marseilles."

The success of *Fiesko* almost surpassed that of *Caesar*. It was well received for twenty-two performances; *Caesar,* meanwhile, still had to be repeated eight more times.

CHAPTER XI

THE THIRD BERLIN ENGAGEMENT

The fame of the Meininger was now established; there remained only the doubt whether they had exhausted their art with what they had already offered or whether they were capable of still greater triumphs. Berlin did not permit its favorites to stand still; they were dropped without pity if they did.

After extending their fame in the same year by guest performances in Vienna and Budapest, the Meininger gave proof of their further abilities when they returned to the capital city in 1876 for their third engagement. They brought with them *Kathy from Heilbronn*[106] and *William Tell*.

The Meininger *Käthchen* was a noteworthy production, not only for its setting, but, more importantly, for its dramaturgy. Up to that time, this jewel of our poetry had been seen only in the mounting which the clumsy hand of Holbein—destroying much of its continuity and most of its beauty—had forced upon it. The Meininger now restored it to its original form. This showed notable courage in a period which still had not become accustomed to seeing offensive things in the theatre or to hearing words that people avoid in good society. These words were, however, much in favor as a manifestation of strength among the men of the Storm and Stress period, just as in the earlier years of the eighteenth century. The Meininger played all those scenes which the revisers had deemed unbeautiful—even immoral.

Kunigunde was seen at her dressing table, rubbing on cosmetics, as a filthy, toothless slut with a nearly bald head, exhibiting only a few strands of hair. When the courtiers appeared, she hobbled away lamely and then later reappeared in her falsely contrived splendor. An amusing and silent by-play was placed between these two scenes. Kleist here directs: "Rosalie, her maid, takes the dressing table and goes." In the Meininger production Rosalie quickly snatched a piece of false hair which she concealed behind her back. Bowing and moving backwards, she then followed her mistress. The audience was also prepared for the mystery of Kunigunde's cosmetic art by the scene in front of the bathing grotto, which up to that time had been cut.

The figure of the Kaiser was again introduced in its fullest development. We may as well confess that the soliloquy in which this high-born

---

106*Das Käthchen von Heilbronn,* a romantic drama of chivalry written by von Kleist in 1810, was the only one of his plays to receive any notice during his lifetime.

gentleman reminds himself of the happy hours of love in Heilbronn, the charming result of which is Käthchen, is extremely ticklish; and the fact that the honest armorer, Friedeborn, is only a fictitious father is founded on a somewhat distressing basis. According to Holbein's precedent, Siegen's revision had also omitted this scene, as did the latest performance at the Deutsches Theater. I believe that such prudery frustrates the intent of the author. The middle-class child must be the daughter of the Kaiser, equal in rank to the noble lover. This is no aristocratic whim of "Gentleman" *von* Kleist; in wanting to see the highest love set in the splendor of the nobility, he is truly reflecting the spirit of the middle ages.

"A great historical chivalric play," so the poet called his work, and to this powerfully romantic note the Meininger production was tuned. The whole play clanged with steel, the brave warriors stamped heavily about in their armor, their talk was loud, they rejoiced in war and were strong in heart. This can be said especially of Josef Nesper. His frank, German appearance was ideally suited to the role of Wetter von Strahl. What a dazzling knightly figure he made!

The Duke had placed the time of the play as that of Maximilian, "the last Knight."[107] It coincided nicely that Weilenbeck, who played the Kaiser, was a speaking likeness of the Dürer picture, with his sharp profile and hawk nose. Entirely free from all sentimentality with which the role could easily be imbued, Adele Pauli played Käthchen. Through her Käthchen, as well as through Weilenbeck's performance as the Kaiser, certainly breathed the great spirit of that fine artist, Baroness von Heldburg.

In order to point out that the art of the Meininger did not rest on the intoxicating splendor of costumes and settings alone, or on the picturesque groupings and the integration of the masses with the action, a homespun slice of life in the Thuringian Forest was produced immediately after this colorful knight's play: Ludwig's *The Forest Warden*.[108] Faithful in the smallest detail to the simple atmosphere of the forester's hut, the masterly ensemble playing earned the same success as the other "propless" plays mentioned before: *The Imaginary Invalid, Twelfth Night,* and *The Learned Ladies.*

On the next night another play of great magnitude was presented: *William Tell*.[109] In the title role Barnay was captivating, although—or perhaps because—his interpretation was very controversial. No one had ever seen such a realistic portrayal of the role. His most illustrious predecessors, Hendrichs and Dettmer, gave it a romantic coloring; they were

[107]The play is laid in the period of Maximilian I (1459-1519), emperor (never crowned) and German king (1493-1519). Because of his chivalrous and slightly quixotic character, he is often known as "the last of the knights."
[108]*Der Erbförster* (literally: *The Hereditary Game Keeper*), written between 1845 and 1849 by Otto Ludwig (1813-1865), shows the author's admiration for Shakespeare's *Othello.*
[109]*William Tell*, first produced in March 1804, was Schiller's last play and the only one to end on a happy note. Based on a combination of history and legend, it is a stirring defense of liberty and the virtues of the Swiss mountain people. Ludwig Barnay, who had caused such a sensation as Antony in the Meininger's opening performance in Berlin, played Tell.

still under the spell of the declamatory school. It was undeniably Barnay's greatest merit that he delved deeply into the characterization of the role, which up to that time had been somewhat mechanically interpreted. In this he was an example to Kainz,[110] who did the same thing for the lover's role.

But this interpretation of Tell[111] as a harmless Alpine hunter, entirely lacking in passion, required a naiveté Barnay did not possess; we saw too clearly the thought that lay behind the portrayal. The calculated effects were obvious to the careful observer. Open to controversy, too, seemed the monologue in the empty path; this was spoken in great haste and agitation. Tell ran back and forth and even threw himself on the ground in order to detect the hoofbeats of the approaching horses. These were the actions of a murderer before his deed, not the behavior of a simple man before a fearfully anticipated step. Later Nesper played Tell. From everything already said about him, it follows that this performance must be numbered among his best.

William Tell is always certain to be a success, since this work of our national poet produces the greatest "German sentiment," a quality on which we consider ourselves to have taken a lease. I must nevertheless confess that in this staging—apart from the interest aroused by the organization of the crowds and the ensemble acting of the people in this frightening play—I find nothing particularly outstanding to raise it above any other good production.

Only the scene with Melchtal was marked by notable artistry. Running parallel to the footlights, a set of narrow steps led to the garret of the hut. Melchtal mounted these steps in order to conceal himself. As soon as the name of his father was mentioned by Stauffacher, he came out from above and with the greatest apprehension began descending little by little. This afforded the actor an excellent opportunity to make use of pantomime.

I must count the Rütli scene as one of the least effective performed by the Meininger. After Stauffacher's speech, a tumult which almost approached that of the forum scene in *Juius Caesar* broke out. According to my view, the uprising of these harshly-oppressed Swiss peasants ought to be shown as something profoundly and inwardly felt rather than something displayed powerfully and outwardly. They are certainly no rioters and conspirators—just men who seek their holy right. My feeling is that even at the first entrance a solemn atmosphere should prevail, like that which the towering silver mountains awaken in every breast. In such an awe-inspiring cathedral one does not shout.

110Josef Kainz (1858-1910), who was to become one of Germany's greatest actors.
111According to the von Müller version upon which Schiller based his drama, the Alpine hunter, Tell, a native of Bürglen in Uri, was a follower of Werner Stauffacher of Schwyz, Walter Fürst of Uri, and Arnold von Melchtal of Unterwalden, but was not a participant in taking the Rütli Oath, sworn in a meadow near Lake Lucerne by these three in preparation for an uprising against the Austrian bailiffs. After Tell's famous feat in shooting the apple from his son's head, he escaped from Gessler, the bailiff, and shot him from ambush near Küssnacht, thus setting off a revolt which ousted the bailiffs in 1308. The scene concerning Melchtal, which Grube believes the Meininger did especially well, relates how the young Melchtal hid in the garret of the hut, but came out of hiding when he overheard that his father had been blinded.

I spoke before about the hoofbeats of the approaching horses. A little slip of the pen: in the Meininger production Gessler and Herras approached on foot; thus Barnay's listening seemed even less justified.

It is undeniable that a horse on the stage, especially if the Gessler cannot ride him, becomes a disagreeable fellow actor; but, on the other hand, it does not seem very dangerous if the Tyrant must say

> Woman, make way
>
> Or my foot will pass over you.[112]

In order to present this scene as Schiller imagined it, the actor playing the governor must not only have a firm seat in the saddle, but Armgart must also possess the courage to seize the reins of the horse, a courage which Rosa Poppe displayed in the highest order. If each of these three, Gessler, Armgart, and the horse, plays his part well (something that does not always happen even in the best theatres), then the scene makes quite a different impression from that produced when Gessler strides along the empty path like any other mortal.

The difficulty of carrying along a good, stalwart, yet handsome-appearing horse or two on these tours would not have troubled the Duke; there was never any question about the expense of such things. Nevertheless, he was a basic opponent of four-footed actors.

After *Tell* had been performed successfully, the Meininger made another attempt to produce an unknown work, but Ibsen's *The Pretenders*[113] proved to be as unsuccessful as Björnson's *Between the Battles* had been. This was partly because the epic style was frequently verbose, partly because the author had created two heroes. Both rivals for the crown, Haakon Jarl and Jarl Skule, are depicted with equal affection and with the same minuteness of detail. The audience can rightly take the side of neither, and that has never been advantageous to theatrical effect. Ludwig's *The Maccabees,* for instance, suffers from this same diffuseness. Juda stands too much in the foreground beside Leah. It seems that even in the theatrical world the Greek expression, "Let there be one king and master," holds true.

The Duke personally lavished much attention on the production of *The Pretenders.* During a journey to Ibsen's northern land—in those days seldom visited—he studied the character of the country closely. A few of his sketches are still extant. There, too, he had found abundance of source material for costumes. The foreign quality shown in this production aroused such wide interest that in spite of the weakness of the play, it ran for seven performances. But it did not find an ultimate response throughout the Empire, as is shown by a careful study of theatre statistics. These ordinarily reflected which plays the Meininger offered in any given year,

112Grube is referring to the last scene in Act IV, where Gessler, the Tyrant, enters on his horse and is stopped by Armgart, a woman whose husband has been unjustly imprisoned. She begs for his life, but Gessler threatens to run her down. It is then she seizes the reins of his bridle. In the Meininger production the Duke's aversion to seeing animals on the stage required that Gessler enter on foot.
113Ibsen's first significant drama (1864). Based on the Norwegian wars of the thirteenth century, it is written in a highly concentrated prose form with but few poetic passages.

since nearly all theatres quickly followed their choices. Through their efforts the classical repertoire regained its popularity, and it would not be an exaggeration to assert that the Meininger re-established the classics for our people.

In the production of *Macbeth,* which followed, again the Meininger aspired to learn as much as possible of its inherent truth. In place of the Schiller version, which was much used in those days, they selected the so-called Schlegel-Tieck[114] translation, which, although it is not the most successful in this collection, does have the merit of following the original text very closely. Better translations, such as that of Gildemeister, for example, were not at that time available.

The Meininger adhered to their principle that as many scenes as possible should be played in the same acting area in order to avoid changing scenery. The first four scenes, for which four different settings are prescribed in the customary Shakespeare edition, were all placed in the same setting, and formed the first act. It is generally known that the indication of place was first inserted by Pope and other editors. The stage in this instance revealed a rocky heath with a rather high knoll visible on the left. Here Macbeth and Banquo entered, while the witches wandered about below. Every time the witches entered, the heavens suddenly darkened. "So foul and fair a day I have not seen."

In the Schiller version, which entirely transformed the three weird sisters, they "appear gigantic and dreadful." In Shakespeare they are "shriveled up": another time they are compared to bubbles, which drift over "the earth as over the water." Schiller let this passage stand although it did not correspond correctly with the earlier description. One would scarcely represent earth bubbles as gigantic. The Meininger witches, played by women, not by men—as sometimes happened then and still frequently does— cringed and crept along the ground. Their grey rags did little to distinguish them from the boulders from behind which they suddenly appeared and then vanished. Grotesque, weird figures came and went. The uncanny atmosphere of *Macbeth* was established in the very first scene.

The rocky platforms from the first act were used in the castle courtyard of the second act, and provided the staircase to Duncan's sleeping chamber. Since the highest scaffolding remained standing, the transformation could be made quite rapidly. As is usually customary, the second act included all the scenes played in the castle courtyard.

As the third act opened in a small room, the change to the banquet scene, which had been set up behind, was accomplished very rapidly. In the diagonal wall to the left a space had been cut out and curtained with scrim. In the opening, which could not be seen until the rear was lighted

---

[114]Ludwig Tieck (1773-1853), German romantic poet, dramatist, and novelist, completed with his daughter, Dorothea, and her husband, Count Baudissin, the Shakespeare translations begun by A. W. von Schlegel. Translated into German idiom of the nineteenth century, the translations did much to popularize the plays of the English poet in Germany.

and the hall in front somewhat darkened, Banquo's ghost appeared. [Plate X A] This solution was not especially successful, particularly since the figure was not visible to everyone sitting on the left. Of course the joint where the edge of the cut-out piece met the heavy canvas was scarcely noticeable, because the gauze had been laid on by degrees and applied more heavily as it approached the edge; yet the joint did remain sharp enough to call attention to the fact that this was a theatrical device. That the ghost did not appear, as usual, in the middle of the stage allowed the audience to observe Macbeth's reactions, since he stood in profile to the viewers.

Without exception the Duke's sets were designed with respect for the actors. To facilitate the play and to heighten its effect always remained for him the most important point. For that reason he never designed any setting merely for its scenic effect; the actor was never compelled to do anything disadvantageous to himself.

In the banquet scene a small set of steps with a graceful balustrade running around the top led upwards from a trap. [Plate X B] Here, with only the upper part of his body visible, the murderer ascended to report his monstrous crime. It was easy for the King to conceal him from the guests with his cloak. As the gloomy figure seemingly emerged from the underworld, it appeared as something horrible.

Banquo's murder was not played on stage—perhaps a mistake. On the other hand, the scene of the outrage on Macduff's wife and little son, a scene which at that time had never been played, was brought on the stage. This scene is frighteningly effective, and it became more so because of its setting: a small room with a set of steps on the rear wall, rising to an upper story. As the mother was talking lovingly with her precocious little son, the audience saw the assassin on the steps above their heads. Step by step, softly but inevitably, their hideous fate approached. The horror of this scene added to the one which followed immediately, in which Ross reported to the unhappy husband and father the dreadful event which the shuddering audience had just witnessed.

Duncan's murder takes place at Inverness; Macbeth's fall, at Dunsinane. The Meininger, nevertheless, played this last scene in the same castle courtyard setting which had witnessed the moonlight scene. It was assumed that the outer ring of walls had been taken by the enemy, and that the battle now raged within the courtyard. The troops of Macduff and Malcolm stormed up the steps. Macbeth, "the hunted bear," burst out the door, and the assailants in confused flight withdrew at the sight of him. On the steps Macbeth fought out the battles with Young Siward and Macduff. The steps were also used effectively for the concluding scene.

CHAPTER XII

THE GUEST TOURS THROUGH 1885

Now the guest tours began through Germany and beyond its borders; these we need not follow, as Paul Richard's statistics in the Appendix of this volume give us the necessary data.

In 1877 an attempt had been made in Cologne to revive Iffland's *The Huntsmen.* The Duke, a fervent huntsman himself, liked the old play, and the head forester and his wife were especially well acted by Hellmuth-Bräm and Frau Berg. But it was a shot that misfired, and after two performances was laid to rest with the dead.

Berlin did not see the Meininger again until 1878, when they brought four new plays back to the capital: *The Robbers, The Prince of Homburg, The Winter's Tale,* and *The Ancestress.*

In every sense, the production of *The Robbers* was an outstanding event. This "lion cub" of Schiller's genius had been both badly treated and neglected. From the first, the court theatres had never been favorable toward it, and hence it had never dared to raise its voice. This youthful work served the great theatres only as entertainment for the gallery gods. Better people went to see it only when some famous star desired to gain cheap applause in the effective role of Franz. On the smaller stages *The Robbers* was given for fill-in performances in which it was completely ruined. People no longer took it seriously, and it became a rich source of theatre anecdotes. That the Meininger wished to revive this "old ham" caused much amazement. How astonished everyone was when the Meininger presented an entirely new play.

First of all, in the setting. Dahlberg,[115] as you all know, wrongly placed the play in the medieval period, a change that was painful to Schiller. In his revision of *The Robbers* the poet complains:

> In the plan of character and plot, the play was laid out as modern; the time has been changed, but the characters and plot remain the same. So we have arrived at something motley-colored like the tights of Harlequin; all the people speak affectedly, and one finds allusions to things neither seen nor allowed until a few hundred years later.

---

[115]Baron Wolfgang von Dahlberg (1750-1806) became in 1778 the able head of the National Theatre in Mannheim. He was a friend of Schiller and presented the first performances of both *The Robbers* and *Fiesko.* Dahlberg showed courage in producing them, for both were very revolutionary for the times. *The Robbers* was set in the medieval period because Dahlberg dared not present it as a play of contemporary life.

At last the Meininger were producing it according to Schiller's demands. In place of the wasp-waists, the elaborate wide coat appeared; the rigid ruff or knight's collar gave way to a graceful lace jabot. [Plate XI A] The Libertines were no longer sixteenth-century foot soldiers, all alike, but became instead members of the Storm and Stress Period, as if they were contemporaries of the poet.

In this new body there dwelt a new soul. The homemade revision by the Mannheim Theatre, which up to that time had held the stage, was discarded. For the first time Germany saw this youthful work of its greatest dramatist in the form in which he had conceived and written it. The role of Franz gained most from the change: he was no longer played as a fantastic scoundrel, a feeble imitation of Richard III. Since the actor was allowed to speak the great monologues which had formerly been blue penciled, he had the opportunity to endow the character with human qualities and to allow it to develop out of the Age of Reason with all its speculation and sophistry.

Still the Mannheim version had one advantage for the stage: the exceedingly effective scenes between Franz, Daniel, and Hermann at the end of Act IV. These were retained. On the other hand, Franz' conversation with Pastor Moser did not prove so impressive. This theological dispute, after Franz has recounted the terrors of his nightmare, seemed like a weak echo. The scene in the last act in which Franz is thrown into the same tower where he had imprisoned his father—this Schiller had certainly regarded as an improvement. "A scene such as the condemnation of Franz has never been seen on the German stage, as far as I am aware," he wrote to Dahlberg. The Meininger, secure in the belief that such obvious poetical justice no longer appealed to our sentiments, returned to the original.

Conversely—instead of "The Song of the Romans," as in the original— they retained the revision of the distant music which Karl Moor demands at the end of Act IV: "Bring your horns and play . . . I must hear soft music, so my slumbering genius may awaken. . . ."

I need hardly mention that the "town councillor" was again turned into a priest. And now how different appeared the figure of Count Maximilian von Moor, to whom again was given the affecting scene in which Amalia reads from the Bible—a scene which up to that time had never been produced. "Old Man Moor,"[116] as the role is still irreverently known today, had in those days generally sunk into a state of absurdity. An actor of any reputation would have rejected it with scorn; therefore it had become the property of those pathetic players of the third and fourth rank. The Meininger gave it to their best actor, Josef Weilenbeck, who well knew how to create a figure of quiet goodness and gentle nobility.

His playing of the scenes in the "Hunger Tower," as they are called in

---

116The melodramatic plot of *The Robbers* concerns two brothers, Karl and Franz Moor, their father, Count von Moor, and Karl's sweetheart, Amalia. The hero, Karl, a young man of good birth and supposedly high motives, turns robber in reaction against a society that will tolerate the injustices he has suffered at the hands of his brother, Franz, a villainous hypocrite. The play is typical of Schiller's early revolutionary period, when he, too, was in revolt against a society he felt unjust.

the theatre, must be designated as highly artistic. He did not fall into the conventional lamentations on which actors in the role had formerly relied— no! The wretched old man, who through his unutterable physical and mental sufferings has fallen into childish senility—a half-mad man—related his terrible story without complaint, but with an occasional foolish smile. The human quality of his undiminished misery was very affecting. Moreover, his appearance supported his interpretation. Even in the most important theatres "Old Man Moor" had been accustomed to stagger forth from the "Hunger Tower" clad in a grey cowl. Audiences paid no attention to the fact that the ruling Count von Moor could scarcely have been laid to rest in such poor clothes—one is not accustomed to entomb an Imperial Gentleman of the Realm in a poorhouse death shroud.

In the Meininger production the pitiable figure wore a parade duty coat, in which the ruler of a small country is usually buried, a lace jabot, and white silk hose. But all this splendor was mouldered, rotten, mutilated, and mangled—a grotesquely terrible appearance! [Plate XI B] In order to produce this effect, the costumer did not use old pieces from the costume room; instead things especially prepared from the best materials were "ruined."

In the old theatre world the cowl generally played a very important part. Anyone who wished to disguise himself had only to put on this universal piece of clothing and he would be recognized by no one. Hermann also traditionally hid himself behind the trusty black cowl when he gave the false report of Karl's death. Besides this, he wore a beard so flagrantly false that viewers in the back of the theatre—not to mention those up close—could recognize it for what is was; but that was the conventional practice. The Meininger did not allow Hermann to enter in a soldier's white cloak, but rather in a bright yellow-grey; for white was avoided as much as possible as not being picturesque. A cloth over one eye and a wig dressed in the military manner made a great difference in the appearance of his countenance. The brightness made his figure the center of the gloomy, somber stage set.

With the "murdering brothers" of the great robber, the gentlemen of the costume room ordinarily did not concern themselves greatly. The robber band received knights' boots and red woolen shirts as far as they were available; then a collection of any shabby costumes had to suffice. With the Meininger, too, a collection of shabby costumes appeared, but for each of these outcasts the Duke had sketched an individual garb. He presented deserters from many branches of the army, Bohemian and Hungarian peasants, depraved students. One wore an expensive embroidered coat, but on his head a rusty helmet; another one had thrown a sacred vestment over his dubious outfit. In short, here was everything thoroughly, artistically, and lovingly thought out to the smallest detail.

When this motley assembly with their freed robber chief stormed down the empty road of the beech forest, gold-laden, singing, whistling, hooting,

roaring—an impetuous mountain stream, an overwhelming flood wave—
the powerful impression created forced the audience to a storm of applause.

After the superabundance of the savagely fermenting forces of *The
Robbers,* there followed that glorification of training and self-discipline,
The Prince of Homburg.[117] This outstanding work had not achieved a permanent place on the stage, however much that great leader of theatrical
criticism, Ludwig Tieck, had praised it. A sleepwalking hero—the symbolism of this paradox had not yet been recognized—and a hero who
could, like any other mortal, succumb to the fear of death, these certainly
contradicted the conventional pattern of the heroic.

In the Meininger production the setting proved to be the strongest ally
of the performances. The loveliness of the moonlight which hovered over
the ivy-clad Fehrbelliner Castle immediately captured the audience by its
charm and conveyed them into a dream-like mood. Then the strongly
arresting military theme brought them back to the reality of the action.

In casting the role of the Princess of Oranien, the Meininger again
departed from the established rule. They did not entrust this part to a
young heroine; on the contrary, they gave it to that actress of sentimental-
naive parts, to the gentle "Käthchen," Adele Pauli. The Duke kept to the
word of the Elector, who repeatedly calls Natalie: "My little daughter,"
"My little niece," "Sweet child"—terms one would hardly apply to a
woman majestic in appearance.

By striving for realistic illusion in this production, the Meininger succeeded in making a slip, the worst that ever occurred to them. The Duke
deemed it necessary that not only should the audience hear the thunder of
the Swedish guns in the battle of Fehrbellin, but also that they should be
able to see the flaming up of the cannon from the Swedish entrenchments,
which stood against the horizon. The so-called miniature fireworks were
set in the upper corner of the stage in front of scenery painted to resemble
a distant chain of hills; with the explosion of these fireworks, a small
bursting cloud of smoke rolled upward. [Plate XII A] A few seconds later,
a great roll of kettledrums was to bring to the audience the sound of firing,
which is of course to be noticed later than the sight of the explosion. On
this piece of business endless time was spent in rehearsal; the proper lapse
between the explosion and the thunder of the cannon would never come
out right. If I am not much mistaken, this annoying business was soon
dropped. At least I don't recall seeing it at the performance which I
witnessed in later years.

The unusually enthusiastic reception accorded to *The Prince of Homburg*
must be credited to the spirit of the times. The memory of the glorious year
of 1870 still flamed in every heart; yet it is equally true that only through

---

117*The Prince of Homburg* (1821) is generally considered von Kleist's masterpiece and
reflects his great admiration for the Hohenzollerns. It has been attacked as narrowly
nationalistic, but it presents a universal love of country in the plot concerning a hero
who is terrified of death, demeans himself, and eventually recovers his honor.

the efforts of the Meininger was this truly patriotic work given a permanent place on the German stage. After the Meininger production every theatre devoted to serious drama took it up. This splendid poem, however, has probably never been more than an artistic success; it still remains caviar to the general.

The role of the Prince was entrusted to young Josef Kainz,[118] whose outstanding talent had been recognized earlier. But this talent was not mature enough for the Berlin critics; Kainz was not able to win the unanimous approval as the Prince which he had won as Kosinski. Blumenthal, the "bloody Oskar" of the Berlin *Tageblatt,* even spoke about "Little Fritz" von Homburg, something the Duke could not forget even years later. When I pointed out to him that the Director of the Lessing Theatre often had to atone for his sins as a critic, he was much pleased at this operation of the laws of compensatory justice.[119]

Still, of all the surprises which the Meininger had offered up to that time, the production of *The Winter's Tale* was probably the greatest. This wonderful play had first been introduced to the German stage by Dingelstedt.[120] As with all of his Shakespearean adaptations, he changed the text at no small cost; and the addition of Flotow's music, somewhat trivial by our present-day tastes, gave to the work an opera-like impression. An elaborate dance with weapons marked the opening; Florizel's reconciliation with his father was portrayed as a pantomime with music; in the pastoral scenes a leaping *corps de ballet* appeared.

But the arts of the opera are still not the narrative arts. I have never received an impression of opera in performances of *The Winter's Tale* in Breslau, in Hannover, or even in the Burgtheater in Vienna. Certainly the antique costumes and settings Dingelstedt used for it were not advantageous; they had something solemn about them. In those days no one had even the smallest knowledge of the joyous colors that animated ancient Greece. The ancients were represented simply as statues of the Glyptothek brought to life; rooms and clothing shone forth in cold whiteness.

Dingelstedt could select this historical period with a show of authority. The Oracle at Delphi definitely intervenes, and the great god Apollo is praised; but we also learn that Hermione is the daughter of the Czar of Russia, and the King of Bohemia—in the Dingelstedt production he ruled over Arcadia—appears. The statue which Pauline wishes to show the bereft Leonates had recently been "finished" by Giulio Romano, "the great Italian master." To cut out all these references in order to preserve an

---

118Kainz was only twenty years old at this time, but before he died in 1910, he had become one of the great actors of Europe. His Romeo and his Hamlet were especially famous.

119Oskar Blumenthal, at first a drama critic, became the director of the Lessing Theatre in Berlin and found that some of the criticism he had directed at others was then leveled at him.

120When Dingelstedt served as Intendant of the Munich Court Theatre (1850-56), he revised everything to his own liking. His careful direction of crowd scenes anticipated the Meininger.

emphasis on the antique was not hard to do. Perhaps Tieck's pertinent remark was in the Duke's mind: "The beginning, middle, and the end of the play should transport the reader into a fairy-tale state of mind in which he gladly abandons and forgets all his historical and geographical knowledge."

The Winter's Tale, as the play is simply known, carries no label as do the other works of the great Englishman—neither a farce nor a comedy, as we may differentiate many of his works which so often swing from the serious to the joyful. The Meininger intended that it should "flit" across their stage as a fairy-tale full of thrills and chills, full of gaiety and joyousness. So conceived, it required above all the magic of color. The Duke conferred on this production the imaginative qualities of the Zaddel costume,[121] known from the pictures of Botticelli. For the King of Bohemia and the shepherds he designed costumes based on their national dress, but freely imagined. In this production generally, in contrast to other productions, he did not lay too much emphasis on historical accuracy; the important thing was that the eye could feast on beauty. He relied hardly at all on the help of music. In the shepherds' dance a bagpipe and a few flutes were heard, but that was all. The Meininger credited Shakespeare with enough skill to weave a magic ring around the audience; therefore, the Dingelstedt version was discarded, and for the first time the poet himself spoke to the German listener. The Meininger were not even deterred by the demand that a bear be brought onto the stage.[122]

The beautiful speech by Time, which Dingelstedt had cut, provided an opportunity for a delightful scene. With an hour glass in her hand the actress rested on a huge terrestrial globe half veiled by clouds.

The court scene [123] was not placed in a hall, but in a free, open place, for Hermione complains that she "has been hurried into the open air":

Here standing
To prate and talk for life and honor 'fore
Who pleases to come and hear.

On the right side they erected a high stage on which were enthroned Leonates, the tribunal, the noblemen, and the women—while a crowd gaped in the background. The watchers who had the greatest share in the action pressed forward on steps and balconies. The heart of the people had long since decided for the chastity of their Queen, even before the message from the Oracle arrived. As the seal was broken and the judgment announced, a universal shout broke out like the sound of thunder: "Let the great god Apollo be praised."[124]

The pastoral festival at the honest old shepherd's hut was idyllic. Here no ladies of the ballet pranced or hopped; the actresses and actors danced in a characteristic rural manner—without perhaps showing any grace,

---

121A medieval garment popular from the twelfth through the fifteenth centuries which had a skirt and sleeves with dagged or foliated edges.
122*The Winter's Tale,* Act III, sc. 3.
123*Ibid.,* Act III, sc. 2.
124André Antoine saw this Meininger production in Brussels and described it in a letter to a friend. S. M. Waxman, *Antoine and the Théâtre Libre* (Cambridge, 1926), p. 96.

yet with natural charm. The dance of the "Saltiers"[125] constituted the height of merriment.

There were in fact "three carters, three shepherds, three neat-herds, three swineherds, that have made themselves all men of hair; they call themselves Saltiers, and they have a dance which the wenches say is a gallimaufry of gambols, because they are not in't; but they themselves are o' the mind,—if it be not too rough for some that know little but bowling,— it will please plentifully."[126]

Well, it did please, although it was a medley of gambols as described. The dance was practiced by twelve soldiers, but their effort was not strenuous; after a few jumps they were allowed to improvise most freely. And these simple but merry young people really outdid themselves in extravagant leaps, somersaults, and tumbles. Finally they formed a chain and began to play leap-frog over each other until the last one, accompanied by applause and laughter, disappeared into the wings. One can scarcely imagine more original, well-made fun.

The final scene was placed not in an enclosed space, but in a garden glowing with color. Among blossoming tropical trees stood a little temple with the statue in it, but not a statue of snow-white marble as in Dingelstedt's Greek world. Instead it was painted several delicate colors, according to the directions of the poet.[127] The painting was just finished; the colors were not yet dry. So, disappearing into fragrance and color, *The Winter's Tale* ended.

From the ranks of the actors Karl Görner merits mention for an outstanding performance. He played the country bumpkin—Dingelstedt called him Mopsus.[128] In 1875 Görner had come to the Meininger as a "bloody beginner," but was soon "discovered." He was a natural born portrayer of "simpletons," a good looking little fellow, full of amiability. Without much talent for characterization, he always played himself, but with original drollness and genuine artlessness. His Launcelot Gobbo was tremendously funny. The art of his comedy was strongly reminiscent of that of Hugo Thimig.[129] Even in appearance these two had a certain similarity, which was all the more noticeable because of the accent of the two Dresdeners— not until later did Thimig abandon his accent. It was as if Nature had published one edition in folio and one in quarto.

The sequence of the plays given in 1878 was especially fitting. After the artistic unrestraint of *The Robbers* came the strict discipline of *The Prince of Homburg;* after *The Winter's Tale,* sunny in spite of its gloomy surroundings, came the terrifying *Ancestress.* This last offering of the

---

[125]Dancers costumed as satyrs.
[126]*The Winter's Tale*, Act IV, sc. 3.
[127]Shakespeare has Pauline say, "O, patience, the statue is newly fixed, the color's not dry," Act V, sc. 3.
[128]Shakespeare calls him simply a Clown.
[129]Hugo Thimig belonged to a notable theatre family which produced many excellent actors, but no great stars.

Meininger might be called their most complete success if—yes, if they had not lent their art to a subject far removed from the material they had been treating up to that time. It is true, of course, that the first fruit of Grillparzer's muse is very rich in theatrical effectiveness, and that may have influenced the Duke in his selection. Besides, one cannot fail to recognize in the Duke a propensity for the gruesome. Laube expressed this same inclination when in his *Burgtheater* he discussed *Othello:* "I demand that the public have nerves." That was also the Duke's idea. We have already observed this when he brought onto the stage the bear scene in *The Battle of Arminius* and the murder of Macduff's little son. Whenever it proved effective to show something in its entirety, nothing was veiled or mitigated. Mitterwurzer said to me once: "Whatever is black, I'll paint black; whatever white, white." At the Duke's productions I was often reminded of this pithy statement of the gifted artist.

Another reason for the selection of *The Ancestress* was that after the great splendor of *The Winter's Tale* the Duke probably wanted to produce a scenically simple piece with only one set change. The problem here consisted solely in holding the audience in one and the same mood for five acts. That, too, was achieved. It is impossible to produce more horror than this production did.

"The thrill of awe is the soul's best part,"[130] says Faust, but in *The Ancestress* the mood is not one of spiritual perception, but of actual physical sensation. The power of this play brought out into the open every fear of the supernatural which in the nineteenth century might slumber in the hidden recesses of the human heart. There were few among the audience whose hair did not stand on end or whose flesh did not creep at the horror of it. By its very dreadfulness this offering stepped out of the frame of the purely artistic; it became a *tour de force* rather than a true work of art. The princely pair, who zealously took the field against anything of the virtuoso in the acting arts, themselves presented in this play a virtuosity in the scenic arts. The production of *The Ancestress* called to mind one of the monstrous but compelling paintings of Wiertz.[131]

Now that I have soothed my aesthetic soul, I must admit that the production was a good one. The setting remained the same throughout the first four acts: a vaulted hall divided into two sections by a row of columned arches.[132] The pattern of the tapestry set on a dull gold background had a peculiar appearance; in the darkness of the chamber it

---

130"Der Schaudern ist der Menscheit bestes Teil." Here Grube is distinguishing between the two meanings of *Schaudern*, the "feeling of dread," and the "feeling of awe."
131Antoine Joseph Wiertz (1806-1865), Belgian historical painter, delighted in complicated, philosophical subjects and scenes from ancient history.
132Laid in a mouldering old castle, *The Ancestress* (1817) tells a Gothic tale of murder, revenge, incestuous love, and supernatural influences. A "fate tragedy," the motivating force is the ghost of the ancestress, who hovers malignantly over the Borotin family, of which only the Count and his daughter survive; the ancestress will not be free until the family is extinct. When Jaromir, a robber, appears one stormy night and falls in love with Berta, the Count does not recognize him as his son and Berta's brother. The action of this dreadful night ends in the death of Berta, and the murder of the Count by Jaromir. When, in the fifth act, Jaromir seeks Berta in the subterranean vaults, he is intercepted by the ancestress and destroyed. She, at last, is free.

seemed—even to a viewer with limited imagination—to shine forth from the wall with almost uncanny faces and figures. Bathed by a glow from the massive fireplace, the aged Count Borotin rested in an armchair. On the heavy oaken table lay an open folio volume, possibly the terrible history of his house, in which even now he had been turning the pages. At his feet knelt his daughter, Berta, in a simple, light grey housedress. [PLATE XII B] The wailing wind swept around the old castle. The conversation of these two was soft; the castle steward who entered did not speak loudly, either. No one did in this house, where something stifling hung in the air.

After his daughter had left and the weary old man had gone to sleep, a strange activity and movement began in the room. As the storm wailed more stridently outside, the light wavered and the fire in the chimney flickered. Now a curious low sound was heard. It seemed as if the wind were driving through broken window panes, as if a sick child were whimpering, or as if a weather-cock were grating as it laboriously turned on rusty hinges. Slowly and noiselessly the heavy door opened—a door which up to that time had been creaking continuously. Berta again entered and the door closed behind her by itself. With inaudible steps she slowly moved toward the old man. But this was not Berta! Nor Berta's soft eyes in the fixed gaze of this "person." Nearer, always nearer, moved the grey figure, and the Count, tortured by his dream, began to groan. He awakened. Still half overcome by sleep, he addressed his daughter. Then he realized it was not she. He shrieked, and the uncanny figure slowly glided to the door, which opened and closed silently. Little by little, still tearing at the nerves, the horrible sound of clanging and groaning and whimpering died away.

But it always began again whenever the ghost was about to appear. It gave a warning, and we kept looking with horror, but still with terrifying curiosity, to see where it was going to appear the next time. Possibly behind the columns, as if it were floating out from the walls! Or was it already standing there behind the easy chair? Oh, if only one did not hear that torturing noise!

It did not seem as if the horror that the ghost engendered could be outdone; but in the last act just that happened in the triple-vaulted burial chamber, into which moonlight streamed through the grated window of the rear wall. Caskets, a ring of them! Caskets, caskets piled one on the other, covered by grey dust. Among them were children's caskets. In the middle a huge sarcophagus covered with dust and tattered blood-red velvet! As once more the whimpering noise began to be heard, the cover slowly, slowly began to rise, and the ghostly figure raised itself bolt upright out of the darkness of the death coffin. Shadowy against the moonlight, which wavered directly behind it, it stretched its arms; the blue-green moonbeams shone through the long sleeves of light gauze. The figure stood there transparent; and after receiving Jaromir in its fatal embrace, the ancestress sank back again into her coffin. The heavy cover sank slowly, slowly back into place. The ancestress had found peace.

After the Berlin appearance in 1878, the group began a series of guest tours within Germany and abroad. The reception in London in 1881 was exceedingly brilliant; the enthusiasm carried over from the production to the players themselves. Societies, as well as private individuals (and certainly not only the members of the German colony), vied with each other in festive preparations to honor the "German Players."

Iphigenia and *Preziosa* had been prepared for the London program. I have little to say about these productions; I know them only from revivals during my management of the Court Theatre.[133] The delicate gossamer dust on the wings of a newly emerged butterfly was understandably somewhat faded.

In *Iphigenia*[134] the usual theatre shackles, which permit their wearer plenty of movement, were replaced by a narrow chain which bound the hands in an awkward position. With the wrists closely locked together certainly no "fine movements" could be executed, but as a result the audience saw real prisoners and realized that they were in great danger. This production, in which Anna Haverlandt played the title role and Barnay, Orestes, achieved a certain theatrical distinction through a noteworthy slip of the tongue. Instead of the words, "I am a man and better it is that I should die," some theatre gremlin put into the mouth of the actor playing Thoas, "I am a woman and better it is that I should die."

As for *Preziosa*[135] this production did not reach the artistic heights of the other works presented, but it was probably selected in order to present to the English audience a performance that was easily understood and at the same time was an example of German folk music. The plan was successful, and *Preziosa* danced across the stage nine times, more often than *Julius Caesar,* which was still the *pièce de résistance.* The English had objected to many things in the Shakespearean production in much the same way that we, in the event that an English company should play Schiller for us, would look upon their efforts. It would probably have been wiser to present a purely German program, but then the problem of comprehension would have been rendered all the more difficult.

The London success secured the world fame of the Meininger, and this they increased through other productions outside of Germany. They later unfurled their banners in Budapest, Graz, Prague, Amsterdam and Rotterdam, Brussels and Antwerp, St. Petersburg, Moscow, Kiev, Odessa and Warsaw, Copenhagen, Stockholm, and Trieste. The journey over "the big pond" was cancelled because of Chronegk's illness.

The Taming of the Shrew was produced in Breslau on September 14, 1881. Curiously and unaccountably, the Meininger discarded their rule of fidelity to the original and used instead the version by Deinhardstein, which had been used earlier at Meiningen and which makes a play already

---

133Grube did not become Intendant of the Meiningen Court Theatre until 1909, more than nineteen years after the company had ceased its tours and when it was no longer "The Meininger."
134*Iphigenia in Tauris* (1787) by Goethe.
135A folk opera (1820) by Pius Alexander Wolff, based on a story by Cervantes.

rowdy even more coarse. This is the only one of the performances I did not see; therefore I cannot give any report on it.

After a break of four years the Meininger returned to Berlin in 1882. This time the demand of the public was so great that they could play not only from April 22 to May 31 in the usual place, the Friedrich-Wilhelm-Städtisches Theater, but also from September 7 to October 15 at the Victoria Theatre, an immense place. The spring engagement brought— besides nine performances of *Julius Caesar,* whose name always remained bound to that of the Meininger—fifteen performances of *Wallenstein's Camp,* of *The Piccolomini,* and of *Wallenstein's Death.*[136]

Even today any theatre would consider the entire production of the whole Wallenstein trilogy as an artistic event. With the Meininger this was even more the case, for they restored to the German stage *The Piccolomini,* which had been almost forgotten. *Wallenstein's Death* formed part of the usual theatre program; and the *Camp* would be given now and then on festive occasions, such as the opening of a new theatre or the arrival of a new stage director. There was a part in this trilogy for every man in the company; and sometimes singers from the opera, who did not disdain such occasions, could participate in the final song. Whenever the larger institutions of art had devoted two nights to *Wallenstein*—and that would be all too seldom—it became evident that the first "lost money," and so *Wallenstein* again temporarily disappeared from the stage. Now people experienced just the opposite. As earlier with *Fiesko,* an almost new play was presented to them.

In the *Camp* there was too much of a good thing; less would have been better, but the motivation of the horsemen's song was praiseworthy. The armorer struck it up on the spur of the moment out of his enthusiasm. Toward the end of the stanza a trumpeter broke in; that gave the trumpeter (the one acting the part in the play) an opportunity to beckon to some musicians in the crowd. A few more kept joining the little chorus until toward the end the singing broke out in full force.

As in *The Prince of Homburg* a military keynote was naturally emphasized, but in the *Wallenstein* trilogy it cropped out more crudely and with less restraint. The first act of *The Piccolomini* illustrated very characteristically the disposition and management of the soldiery.

> "Even in the town hall, I see you have
> Already made yourselves pretty much at home,"

says Isolani. To be sure, this accommodation was not very comfortable. A chest had been broken open. Bundles of documents lay on the floor; and it was not taken amiss, but considered very natural, when Max contemptuously kicked aside a roll of papers with these words:

---

[136]The *Wallenstein* trilogy (1799-1800) by Schiller, is divided into a prologue, *Wallensteins Lager,* and two five-act dramas, *Die Piccolomini* and *Wallensteins Tod.* The hero of the trilogy is the historical Count Albrecht von Wallenstein (1583-1634), commander of the Imperial forces in the Thirty Years' War.

". . . The General needs
Every greatness of nature;
He should not question lifeless books, old orders
Nor mouldering documents."

In the corner lay some captured Swedish drums with their blue and yellow streamers; banners and standards stood about everywhere, and muskets leaned against the wall. The bare and darkened hall was not "decorated" as Schiller prescribes, but instead offered a picture of rude army life.

The banquet in the fourth act was a sight worth seeing. Faithful to the modern principle of omitting everything which might divert the attention of the audience from the performers, Jessner[137] in his *Wallenstein* production in the Berlin State Playhouse (performed incidentally to the greatest applause) did not bring the banquet of the generals on to the stage. It was not Schiller's intention to omit this scene, for he set forth in detailed instructions how this scene should be staged, and the Meininger followed these instructions faithfully. The poet's intention was to make the "wine-tipsy" atmosphere, in which the confiding Illo arranged his clumsy plan, apparent and believable. To be sure, it is hard, very hard, if one follows Schiller's instructions, when "everyone is moving about," to give the proper attention to the words of the play. Yet, naturally enough, this was all-important to the Meininger.

When Adolf Winds in his work mentioned above professed not to have received this impression, this fact must be laid to the performance on that particular evening. Although Chronegk superintended all the performances without exception with untiring zeal, of course it cannot be asserted that at every performance the same high standard was attained. A let-down almost never occurred, even on hot summer evenings, but occasionally the enthusiasm of the young actors in the crowd scenes grew to over-enthusiasm.

The climax of the play, the end of the third act with the sudden attack of von Pappenheim's cavalry, afforded the most splendid incident in the production, and rightly so.

Even in the best theatres the "storm" of this attack was accustomed to attain a velocity of only four or five miles an hour. Indeed I have often seen these rebel warriors arranged in rank and file marching at a moderate speed in goose-step, like organized troops. The first row usually had armor and helmets, but that would have exhausted the average theatre armory. Therefore, those following appeared in ugly yellow "leather" trousers, usually made of cloth.

All the Meininger armored cavalry wore the correct Pappenheim equipment, the blackened breastplate. Like an iron sea the mass of men, armored from head to foot, rolled one after the other in waves across the steps of the entrance to the hall. [Plate XIII A] Each newly attacking man tried to

137Leopold Jessner (1878-1945) became director of the Berlin *Schauspielhaus* in 1919 and created there one brilliant and eccentric success after the other. In *William Tell* he introduced the famous "Jessner steps," which dominated his early settings.

press forward and to push back those standing in front of him. But these did not wish to give up their places, and tried to retain the lead. In any case, the multitude never stood still; it was in continual agitation. Every trooper struck with frenzy against those who had come first; and with each assault there was a clanging of iron.

Naturally, there were no supers in the first ranks, but young actors; not a dull or indifferent face appeared there; grimness and menace glowered beneath each helmet. Swords flashed, the shouts became louder and wilder as the Pappenheim attack increased from without. The force of the crowd —the elemental violence! Who would have had any doubt that Max[138] must have been carried away by this wave.

Alexander Barthel, who unfortunately was to die of a malignant liver disease in his youth, played the young hero just as one would imagine him. A rather delicate, mischievous, handsome appearance was joined to a fiery temperament—for which a musical voice assured every means of expressiveness. As Max he never lost himself in sentimentality; he remained (to be sure, influenced by the spirit of the play) always "the son of the camp." The apostrophe to peace, easily leading to sickening sweetness, became in his mouth no fanatical-sentimental tirade; he spoke it in a tone of one joyfully astonished over things he had never imagined before that moment. The *Wallenstein* cast in general was worthy of mention. Next to Nesper's magnificent, although to my mind too gentle, Wallenstein, stood the spirited Terzky of Marie Schanzer, later Frau von Bülow; and the Meininger possessed two excellent portrayals of Illo and Isolani in Karl Weiser and Wilhelm Arndt. These two talented men would have held the promise of great careers if good fortune had provided them training and education. The time in which talent alone was enough to insure a first place in the theatre was long since past—to the advantage of the theatre, to the disadvantage of many individuals.

Karl Weiser, also very gifted as a poet, but hampered by a lack of self-criticism, offered as Illo a performance which compared favorably with that of Munich's Hausser. His strongest point lay in that kind of role which demands a certain brutality. He was, for example, an outstanding Engstrand in *Ghosts*. But he preferred himself in the ideal heroic roles such as Brutus and Leonates. He carried a handsome, interesting head on his somewhat massive body, but his acting in heroic roles was marred by a hoarse voice, a defect which all his art of speaking could not entirely cover.

Wilhelm Arndt's Isolani was a figure which impressed itself unforgettably upon the memory. In a brownish-yellow face, which was rimmed by white hair and with which the black brows and long black hanging mustache contrasted strongly, flashed two daring yet cunning eyes. The body of the old cavalryman rested on two crooked legs. The artist carried off this characteristic detail so cleverly that once I heard somone say: "That Arndt is a distinguished actor; too bad he has bow-legs."

[138]Octavio Piccolomini was an historical character, a general in the Imperial forces during the Thirty Years' War. In the drama, Schiller gave him a non-historical son and rival, Max, who was in love with Wallenstein's daughter.

His Isolani was jovial, but still somewhat awkward in movement, to some extent uncertain in behavior, as one who cannot find his way entirely in a strange environment. For all that, he was, however, still a count; and one never forgot the great cavalry leader, that important personality whose defection brought the first heavy blow upon the Friedlander.[139]

To Bremen, which had already seen the first performance of *Wallenstein's Camp* on May 18, 1881, the Meininger brought on May 22, 1883, Fittger's *The Witch* as an added proof that not only the revival of classical stage treasures lay close to the heart of the Duke. It was also proof of the great intelligence of an unusual Duke who recognized no limitations for the repertoire of a Court Theatre.

If *Pope Sixtus* and *The Massacre of St. Bartholomew* were—with their partly anti-clerical or at least their freethinking tendencies—not "Court Theatre pieces," *The Witch* touched with a much bolder hand on questions of faith. Thalia, the heroine, the mistress of a Frisian castle, waited ten years for her betrothed, who as a general had to experience the terrors of the Thirty Years' War. During this time she applied herself to philosophical studies under the guidance of a Jewish tutor whom she had rescued from persecution. These studies had estranged her from the beliefs of the church. The climax is played in front of the church in which Thalia's marriage is to be celebrated.

The peasants, stirred up by an officious Jesuit and a fanatical Protestant, consider Thalia a witch and demand menacingly that she be required to clear herself of the suspicion by swearing on the Bible. "I love these pages," she cries out, "as the most noble devised by the spirit of man, but you wish to make them chains for me . . . I shall break the chains!"

Of course, the Bible was not torn up on the stage; the Meininger working text directs: "She throws the Bible from her," but in those days even to perform that act on the stage was a risky thing. In passing we should acknowledge that Pollini in Hamburg possessed enough courage to play this tragedy for the first time. But it first found its way into theatres across Germany through the Meininger.[140]

There was nothing special about the production or the setting to discuss. Primarily Chronegk's direction was excellent, and it goes without saying that the mass scenes were outstanding. An entirely unusual error of direction, which strangely enough was overlooked by the critics, crept in: in the winter scene at the cemetery we observed many peasants in their shirt sleeves.

Artur Fitger,[141] the painter-poet whose perfectly composed, profoundly thoughtful, and deeply tender lyric of northwestern Germany is only little

---

[139]*i.e.*, Wallenstein, who was the Count of Friedland.
[140]They later played it in Berlin, Vienna, Breslau, Prague, Leipzig, Graz, Mainz, Trieste, and Dresden. It had been written in 1879.
[141]Artur Fitger (1840-1909), author of this lyrical play, *The Witch*, which the Meininger admired greatly. The public did not receive it with enthusiasm.

known, soon became a friend of the ducal pair, who had him to thank for much worthwhile stimulation.

As a curtain raiser for *The Imaginary Invalid* from that time on, the Meininger presented the amiable, gossipy play, *Lydia,* by Gensichen, which was given for the first time in Mainz on May 5, 1884. *The Crucifix Carver from Ammergau* was also presented there for the first time. By chance there were many southern Germans in the troupe acquainted with the dialect, but still the performance suffered unfavorably in comparison with that of the Munich players. It was repeated only eleven times; later, in 1890, another blunder was *'S Nullerl*[142] by Morre, which fitted even less into the Meininger frame. They gave it probably because of the outstanding acting of Adolf Link as Anerl, which in its touching simplicity could compare with that of Schweighofer. This folk play was shown only once in Moscow and then in Odessa.

In 1882 the Meininger brought *Maria Stuart*[143] to Berlin in a production on which I must tarry again for awhile. How the Meininger splendor, which naturally found its richest opportunity at the court of Elizabeth heightened the impression of the play! How drab by contrast was the effect of the barren walls at Fotheringay! How clearly was shown to the audience the grim hatred with which Elizabeth pursued the Queen who demanded the right to drive her out of those royal halls! How one felt Maria's profound humiliation!

Elizabeth's entrance in the second act was remarkably impressive. [Plate XIII B] It had become customary in most theatres to cut the short conversation between Davison and Kent; although quite apart from the interesting content of this conversation, it is very necessary to see both of these characters, for the speech of Davison is really important, while Kent gives a significant summary of the tragedy. The Meininger again produced this seemingly unessential scene and gave up the brilliant opening scene with the Queen on her throne surrounded by her court.

Instead they created for her a scene never before produced in this manner. After Davison's words:
> "She goes into the bridal chamber,
> The Stuart goes to her death,"
they introduced splendid march music, in which a major part was given to the drums. And then we saw something unusual: before Her Majesty, the entire court entered the hall—all the while bowing and moving backward, for they were not permitted to turn their backs to the face of the Queen.

The Duke related to me how strongly this point of ceremony was

---

[142]*i.e.,* "Nobody."
[143]*Maria Stuart* (1801) relates the story of Scotland's unhappy Queen in terms of personal rivalry between her and Elizabeth. Much of Schiller's early violent anti-Catholicism, which was so evident in his youthful work, *Don Carlos,* had been tempered by the years, and he could treat the problems of Catholicism and its influence on governments in an objective and impartial way.

observed in London even in his time. He was once a witness when at a solemn reception an embassy group unfortunately missed the door and found itself in a corner of the hall, so that it cost the company present great pains to keep from laughing. Only a stage director like the Duke who did not need to say as Davison did, "I know not the speech of courts and kings," could have hit upon this particular entrance.

This kind of entrance was not without difficulty for the lords of the court, especially Shrewsbury and Burleigh—who, as well as Leicester, were clad in the robes of Knights of the Garter, a long red velvet garment, which was covered by a voluminous blue velvet cloak. Once in Munich this monster led to the only unintentional laughter that the Meininger ever had to experience. The actor playing Leicester, a very tall gentleman, stumbled against the high steps on which the throne stood; and we suddenly saw a pair of endlessly long, white-clad legs projecting heavenward from billows of velvet.

The garments of the court members were rich, yet heavy, and fashioned in dark colors. As soon as the courtiers had formed a line on each side, twelve pages, blazing in gold and white, appeared; they were not turned toward the Queen, since they were part of her immediate entourage, but were stepping lightly and straight ahead. Then, at last, the Queen entered, led by Leicester.

After the Queen (at whose entrance everyone had sunk to his knees) had mounted the throne, she gave a little signal, whereupon the court was again permitted to arise. [Plate XIV A] Now came the elegant, almost dandified French ambassador, clad in bright satin material, the cut of which was entirely different from the heaviness of the English style.

The conferring of the Order of the Garter was also presented as a little ceremony appropriate to the high honor of this award: Burleigh and Shrewsbury led Count Bellièvere before the Queen, and the whole court fell to one knee. Everything breathed courtliness, royal pomp, and regal power.

On entering as well as on leaving the royal chamber everybody had to fall to one knee; even the high dignitaries were obliged to observe this standard of the strict court etiquette.

The setting for the garden scenes was not free from criticism. It is obvious from Schiller's words that he meant us to see a joyous landscape, a seemingly fortunate escape from the "dreary prison," the "unhappy vault." To be sure, the more gaily the scenery symbolizes the innate hope of the unlucky Queen, the more frigid becomes the air when her enemy enters the park. The Meininger believed that they must hold fast to the basic somber tone of the tragedy; the encounter of the Queens took place in a low avenue of beeches, which arched overhead in the brown-red colors of autumn.

Elizabeth's action in signing the death warrant was wonderfully strengthened by the black-floored chamber, illuminated only by the light of two silver candelabra placed on a writing table. The great picture of Henry VIII in a white, gold-embroidered coat glared down from the dark background

—almost like a ghost. The tyrant, who had approved so many bloody judgments, seemed to smile down on his daughter.

No less important an artist than Artur Fitger had reproduced the portrait, which was based on that of Holbein.

The last act was a masterpiece. It was played in the same barren room which had already evoked a chill in the first act. A huge door, which had remained unused in Act I, occupied the largest part of the back wall. It opened for the first time as Maria was about to go to the scaffold and disclosed a view of a staircase wall. [Plate XIV B] Walls and balustrades were hung with black.

The outer room was occupied by soldiers who separated the ladies-in-waiting from the Queen, and with halberds and muskets drove them—sobbing loudly and sometimes shrieking hysterically—across the upper stairs, while Maria, doomed to death, descended.

> "Under my feet
> The terrible deed is being carried out,"

said Leicester later.

Accompanying this nerve-wracking scene, the music of a brass band intoned an unusually sharp, austere rhythm. Chronegk explained that the music was the "Witches' March," which was played at the burning of a Striga[144] and which Elizabeth, out of scorn, had ordered to be played at Maria's execution. The accuracy of this must be questioned; we possess many facts about the execution of the sentence, but nothing is said of any such music.

In Maria's costuming, the Duke deviated from Schiller's descriptions. The "white dove in a flock of crows," to quote the words of Romeo, seemed to him too allegorical as well as not really picturesque. He confined himself rather to contemporary reports, which of course did not speak uniformly on this point; nevertheless, they did agree that the Queen was dressed magnificently but soberly as she walked to her death. Brantôme,[145] who always displays the greatest interest in the dress of the Queens of his time, speaks about the entirely black velvet dress, the only one that still remained to her. Although he calls on the testimony of two eye-witnesses from the suite of the Queen, he produces here the impression that he wished always to arouse sympathy for the heroine of his *discours troisième*.

The final scene, up to that time almost always cut, was again restored. This has continued as the custom to the present day.

Marie Schanzer (Frau von Bülow) was a spirited Elizabeth; and Olga Lorenz a touching sufferer as Maria, but one in no way lacking in royal majesty. Both of these ladies were very good portrayers of Marwood and

---

144An Italian sorceress of the medieval period.
145Pierre de Bourdeilles, seigneur de Brantôme (1535?-1614), French courtier, soldier, and author of famous memoirs. Among his other exploits he accompanied Mary Stuart to Scotland. His memoirs, including his *Livre des dames,* published in two parts as *Vies des dames illustres* and *Vies des dames galantes,* form a racy and vivid account of his time.

of the title role of *Miss Sara Sampson*.[146] This drama, as the Meininger called it—why is not apparent, since Lessing calls it a tragedy—found, as a matter of course, a respectful reception and offered new proof that the Meininger did not rely on spectacular effects alone.

For the engagement at St. Petersburg in 1885 *The Bride of Messina*[147] was rehearsed. This production was carefully prepared, but it was not in any way outstanding.

---

[146]*Miss Sara Sampson* (1755) by Gotthold Ephraim Lessing (1729-81) was a reworking of the Medea story in an English middle-class setting.
[147]Schiller's *Die Braut von Messina* (1803) was patterned after Sophocles' *Oedipus Rex*. It is not numbered among his greatest plays.

CHAPTER XIII

THE LATER GUEST TOURS

Early in 1886 negotiations with America were in full progress. I have this projected tour to thank for being able to return to the Meininger in the role in which I had made my first (and not entirely successful) stage appearance. The engagement in New York, after which a tour through the States was to follow, was never realized. Chronegk, whose French was excellent, but whose English was not so strong, felt an aversion to placing himself entirely in the hands of an agent. He demanded guarantee upon guarantee until the American agent, wearied by the long negotiations, broke them off. Probably Chronegk also realized that he was no longer equal to the exertion of an enterprise of several months' duration. In Düsseldorf in the fall of the same year he suffered the stroke which he had been dreading. Paul Richard carried on to the end of the engagement with industry and prudence. If Chronegk had suddenly broken down in the middle of a tour through America, the consequences would have been incalculable; he was the soul and the moving spirit of everything.

But I was already in Meiningen, promised what was considered in those days a very high salary, and roles had to be found for me.

First of all, *The Merchant of Venice* was again undertaken and cast into entirely new form. Nothing remained of the 1874 production. It was as if the Duke wished to show what he had learned in the meantime.

This was a strange Ghetto, with its dilapidated houses, its ragged washing hanging from lines stretched over the streets! A canal, spanned by a bridge, ran transversely across the stage. Taken over by Reinhardt, this arrangement has become traditional on the German stage and is still found frequently in present-day productions. While the gondola with the escaping Jessica departed beneath the bridge, the masqued procession about which Launcelot Gobbo had chattered frolicked over it.

At the first Berlin rehearsal a sketch by Steinle was taken as a basis for the court scene. It suggested that possibly the throne for the Doge could be placed at the side of the stage. Up to this time it was an unbroken rule that Lords must always have the middle of the stage for their basic position. Quite correctly, this was considered the most effective place an actor could take, since it provided him an opportunity to speak directly to the front and to turn his full face to the audience. It is true that the middle does belong to the Prince if he is the leading actor, as for instance in the first act of *Lear;* but in this scene of *The Merchant of Venice* attention should be directed to Portia and Shylock, not the Doge. If he is in the middle, then the actor portraying the Jew must speak with his back to the audience. If he assumes a natural position or if he takes an unnatural three-quarter position, which injures the truth of the play, it is hard to render the correct illusion. For one naturally faces a person to whom he is speaking, especially if he is standing before a court.

The expressionistic[148] school, to be sure, does not hold that opinion, and now the Doge is again usually placed in the middle of the stage. It makes a more beautiful picture, since today parallelism is considered an ideal of beauty, and since at the present time the stage is ruled more by the painter than the actor.

The painter Georg II was of a different opinion, and so on the whole the basic plan of the early design remained unchanged. I must praise another scenic effect less—or rather, not at all. On the back wall, which was placed somewhat diagonally, was a gallery (or more accurately, a long loggia) filled with spectators, men and women, who followed with interest the proceedings of the court. It is true that it did produce a wonderful impression during Portia's plea for justice when this circle of observers broke out with loud handclapping into a wild jubilation of applause and when it later greeted Gratiano's jeering speech with laughter. But this effect could also have been produced if the spectators had been crowded into the background. Hanging as they did directly over the heads of the performers, they called too much attention to themselves. For this reason it was an unnecessary touch. The inclusion of the public could indeed have been omitted altogether.

It is easier to praise the Italian street scenes which were presented between the individual acts of this production, although nowadays these scenes would be cut. Even here the production went astray; for instance, these included the poorly dressed man who even today helps in landing gondolas with a long stick tipped with a nail. I felt that this silent figure who participated in no portion of the action was really annoying. On the other hand, the setting in the last act offered an impressive picture with a replica of the Villa Carlotta, which belonged to the Duke. This production enjoyed much success in the new staging. In the course of four years it was repeated ninety times in guest engagements.

The second big part given to me was Byron's *Marino Faliero.*[149] Artur Fitger had translated and adapted this play, to which Goethe previously had alluded. How Goethe handled the stage details is not entirely clear from the passage in Eckermann:[150]

"If it were still my business to superintend a theatre," says Goethe,

[148]Grube defines this term in his Preface.
[149]Lord Byron's *Marino Faliero* (1820) is a tragedy concerning fourteenth-century Doge of Venice, the conspiracy in which he had a part, and his trial and punishment by death.
[150]Johann Peter Eckermann (1792-1854), German scholar and author. He assisted Goethe in various literary labors, was professor of literature and German at Jena, and librarian at Weimar. He quoted many of the poet's opinions in his *Conversations With Goethe* (1836-1848).

"I would, for example, bring the Doge of Venice on to the stage. To be sure, the play is too long, and it should be shortened; but one cannot just snip and cut. On the contrary one must do this: he must determine the meaning of each scene and then merely reproduce it in a shorter way. By this means the play would become shorter without being ruined by alteration; and it would gain a more powerful effect without losing its essential beauty."

It seems as if Goethe had thought of some sort of reworking; Fitger had restricted himself to cutting—which, however, was not sweeping enough. Also a more thorough revision could hardly have breathed dramatic life into this poetically important work. Grillparzer hit the mark with his judgment:

> Byron's Faliero is too vacillating. Such characters are in no way unsuitable for tragedy; on the contrary, they are of the highest order, but there must be something else in the tragedy besides them, something well established which provides a nucleus for the whole and gives it significance. In Byron's tragedy there is nothing of the sort. He failed to establish the state of Venice and its judicial system as such a center of interest—which would have been an obvious choice—and, therefore, the play as a whole lacks dramatically strong action, as well as Aristotelian unity of action.

Frau von Heldburg had taken a special fancy to the play. I have some ground for the assumption that she stimulated her friend to translate it. Perhaps she perceived her own husband in the figure of the youthfully robust old man, Faliero; and probably the play called to mind also much slander and wrong which had been inflicted upon her when her own marriage aroused such prejudice and jealousy. The Duke warmly undertook this drama that his wife liked so much. He probably never created more intoxicating pictures than appeared in this play.

In Mainz, where on May 12, 1886, the first performance was given, the success was marked, and in the artistic center of Düsseldorf the reception became frankly enthusiastic. With joyful expectations the Meininger brought the play into Berlin the next year—only to experience a great disappointment. There they had already trained the Berliners much too well; "retouched pictures" were no longer enough.

As long as Botho von Hülsen held sway, it is true that the Royal Playhouse had been completely closed to modern methods, but the newly rising Deutsches Theater moved with full sails into the Meininger channel. Nearest to the outstanding ensemble and the modern program of the Meininger were Barnay's and Forster's productions, which drew universal approval to the new stage. It was with these that L'Arronge allied himself. But not until Count Hochberg became director of the Royal Playhouse was any allowance made in this theatre for the trend of the times. He himself then staged performances of the *Wallenstein* trilogy and of *Maria Stuart* which were certainly overrich and here and there a little "vulgarized."

In any case, and especially through these, he had again drawn attention to the royal stage, which had fallen into considerable disrepute.

Therefore, the Meininger had to offer something extraordinary if they wished to claim a victory.

They did offer something extraordinary in *The Maid of Orleans*. The somewhat overworked expression, "They surpassed even themselves," is here really to the point.

It is a remarkable coincidence that the Meininger in their last engagement in Berlin, just as in their first, should bring to the stage a distinguished new theatrical talent. At the beginning and at the close of the Meininger guest performances Ludwig Barnay and Amanda Lindner stand as two armor-bearers.

Barnay, who was already well known in the theatre world, but who with his Marc Antony became universally famous, had been brought to the Meininger by an agent. They themselves "discovered" Amanda Lindner. If Barnay may be designated as a prototype of manliness, animated by strength and spirit, then one must consider Amanda Lindner as a true ideal of maidenly beauty, possessing a stage presence such as has been granted to very few.

A tall, slender figure, a face of classic mold, great gentle eyes, which could nevertheless blaze up with enthusiasm, a low, ingratiating alto voice—all this had been bestowed on her by a kind nature.

The extraordinary merit of Baroness von Heldburg is that she recognized in this unusually talented girl a vessel into which she could pour her own inspiration—or, to use Goethe's phrase, an inspired instrument through which the great artist could speak. The Meininger, or rather we should say Helene von Heldburg, gave to the stage through Amanda Lindner a new comprehension of Schiller's wondrous maid. [Plate XV A]

The greater a poetic figure is, the more many sided it usually is, and the more contradictory are the things said about it by itself and by others. The art of the actor must bring a unity to these seeming contradictions. Immediately, Hamlet comes to mind. How many interpreters of the role differ in their views, and yet, who really cares about that after all, if a true artist is capable of making the role truly human.

Joan of Arc is one of these many-sided characters. Every person in the play judges her differently. That is not really very puzzling; even the importance of lifeless things is interpreted differently by different people. The oak which overshadows the setting in the first scene is to the black-blooded father Thibaut the "Druid tree from which all lucky creatures flee;" he himself has seen a sinister magic spirit there. But for Joan it is a holy oak, and under its branches the Mother of God appears.

Joan, the shepherdess of innocent lambs, often calls herself the frail maiden and speaks about the tender soul of the shepherdess. But this tender soul not only subdues the tiger wolf; she also conquers and destroys heroes. Is there not an insoluble contradiction here? Still only one interpretation could be presented, and up to that time the decision had been for the heroic spirit. Klara Ziegler became the celebrated "Jungfrau," she who might assert without boasting about herself: "I bear a thunderbolt in my mouth," she who towered almost a head over all those standing about her. Every one of Joan's heroic acts became conceivable, but "to be sure, it was no longer a miracle."

For her interpretation Helene von Heldburg sought the miraculous, and by that means she hit upon the correct one. Only in her interpretation could the contradictions in the role be reconciled. Before that time too little attention had been paid to the fact that the poet called his tragedy a romantic one. This legendary, marvelous quality shone out of Amanda Lindner's performance with compelling beauty. She did not merely speak; a higher voice spoke through her. She walked forth as in a dream, and now and then—this was especially touching—she seemed to waken partially and be astonished at herself and to be frightened.

The success which the entirely unusual interpretation enjoyed is too well known to need any more special attention called to it. If today the actress of Gretchen and Klärchen may also make a claim for the role of Joan, she has the Meininger to thank for that.

Even though Frau von Heldburg had understood the soul of the work and had awakened it to new life, it was the Duke who gave it a most beautiful body. The whole mystical charm of Gothic architecture seemed to have descended upon the stage through the wonderful colors of the church windows, adapted from the paintings of the old masters. The princely director, who was at the same time his own "artistic adviser," had never bestowed more exhaustive research, greater expenditure of talent, or a more sincere study upon the intentions of a poet. With what earnestness and what conscientiousness the Duke was accustomed to go about his work is illustrated, among other things, by the fact that he produced seven different designs for the prologue of *The Maid of Orleans*.

The difficulty lay in bringing the little chapel close to the unholy Druid tree, at the same time showing the meadows which Joan tended and from which she took leave with such a heavy heart. A proper design should combine into one symbolically effective picture the simple innocence of a smiling land untouched as yet by the horrors of war, but one a prey to dark superstitions and one to which its deliverer must be sacrificed. The Duke finally succeeded when he placed the little chapel entirely in the foreground and the forbodingly melancholy magic oak in the middle, while to the left a distant view opened on a charming valley through which a meandering water course threaded its way and by which lay a friendly little village in the distance. [Plate XV B] In those days one slaved over such questions, while today he need only lower the cyclorama.

The most interesting point of the production, of course, took place at the coronation, but not by means of the splendor with which Iffland had dazzled the Berliners; the emphasis in this case was laid on the constantly increasing enthusiasm of the crowd. [Plate XVI A] Head to head they pressed into a rather narrow street — it has already been mentioned repeatedly that the Meininger knew how to give an impression of great masses by contracting the stage space. They also accomplished this by having the crowd not only stand on the stage but extend into the wings, so that the audience could not see the edges of it. People looked out of all the windows, filled up the narrow staircases to the house doors, and climbed onto the Gothic fountains. Joyful excitement ran through the crowd as soon as Dunois or some other honored and beloved general came into view. At last, as the King entered the square under his canopy, the trumpeters on the dais at the entrance to the cathedral, which cut across the background, sounded a fanfare on their long trumpets. Thereupon, there arose a shout of jubilation which would seem impossible to surpass. And yet just that happened as the national heroine came into view. [Plate XVI B] There broke out a frenzy of almost indescribable excitement, which irresistibly swept every member of the audience along with it.

Let me here at last disclose a particular trick of the director. For the music accompanying the procession, parts of Brahms' Variations on Hayden's "Chorale of St. Antony" were selected—of course, in the simplest instrumentation. Because of the fact that its melody appeared again and again—it seemed never to stop, so to speak—the impression of a certain endlessness was carried over with respect to the procession, which appeared to last much longer than really was the case.

It has already been mentioned that the Duke had a predilection for staging warlike scenes. Here there was no want of such scenes. The attack on the English camp in the second act always constituted a cross for the director of a realistic production. Here again the Meininger principle of narrowing the stage proved itself. "A place circumscribed by rocks," read Schiller's directions. The Meininger placed the rocks around a steep defile. As the curtain rose, we saw the weary rear-guard of the defeated English forces streaming down the narrow opening in the row of rocks. Several horsemen were trying to drag out of this place a huge, unyielding wagon with all sorts of rescued army goods. They succeeded in doing so, but only as far as the right foreground. Then, their strength completely gave out; they collapsed and sank swiftly into deep sleep. Gradually the stage emptied and the generals could begin their conversation. This wagon was in no way merely decoration; its purpose was later to mask the greatest part of the attacking French soldiers, so that one could not accurately gauge their number. At the same time, its movement by the soldiers brought concretely before the eyes of the audience the utter exhaustion of an army in headlong retreat.

"Station good watchmen; occupy the heights," commanded Talbot, who was skilled in war. But it was clear to the audience that these soldiers, tired to death, could furnish no effective guards, nor could they offer any real opposition to an attack.

The incident of Talbot's death presented a touching scene. Heavy

· 107

low-hanging black clouds, only a harsh, yellow streak on the horizon through which the distant gloomy towers of Rheims Cathedral rose! To the right and somewhat to the back, there was a ruined cottage with charred rafters, and a mighty cannon barrel without the gun carriage, resting on a low wooden rack. A shed was larded with arrows. The wounded and the dead lay on the battlefield—this last, one should remark in passing, was a Meininger innovation; up to that time audiences were led to believe that in battles of former days human life was never lost. Somewhat to the middle Talbot lay against his warhorse, cut down by an arrow. [Plate V A]

In the ruins mentioned above, the "Black Knight" disappeared with the aid of a cleverly contrived folding contraption; for—apart from the fact that one could not be sure of finding trap doors in the right places on every stage—the Duke was an avowed opponent of traps. He simply would not accept that square hole covered by a lid—even though, to be sure, it can always be concealed from the people in the orchestra by a little piece of scenery. In other plays, too, whenever a figure had to disappear suddenly, he would solve the problem in some other way.

Yet the Meininger cannot be spared a reproach for the way in which they handled the appearance of the Black Knight, for they were quite unjustified in not remaining true to their basic principle of reverence to the poet's intention. They allowed the Black Knight to be played by an actor other than the one playing Talbot—a decision which was entirely against the thought of the play and Schiller's expressed wish. As he said in a letter to Goethe: Talbot as an atheist is doomed to hell.

The final scene was effective; distant music of the spheres vibrated through the twilight sky, against which the flags were silhouetted. As these sank down and covered the dead, the bright evening sky became visible, and the last warm rays of the sinking sun seemed to point upward to "everlasting joy."

As brilliant as the beginning of the Meininger guest engagements was their conclusion. Fifty-five performances of *The Maid of Orleans* in Berlin were followed by 139 others in Germany and abroad within the next four years. Schiller's romantic tragedy was the swan song of the Meininger.

Of the plays that followed, only Echegaray's *The Great Galeoto*[151] was a strong theatre success. This drama, unusually appropriate for the taste of those days, was performed everywhere in Germany.

Two others that followed, *Alexandra* by Richard Voss and Fitger's *The Roses of Tyburn,* managed to win only moderate applause. It was because of their friendship for the authors that the Meininger presented these particular plays. The princely pair willingly suspended all criticism for their friends; and during and after the time of the guest engagements, the Meininger gave many performances for which there was no pressing neces-

---

[151] Miguel Echegaray (1832-1916) wrote *El Gran Galeoto* (1881) while under the influence of Ibsen. This is a thesis play concerning the effects of gossip on an innocent family.

sity. In particular Paul Heyse's unsuccessful struggle for the wreath of the dramatic muse was most lovingly supported every season.

But a production which could be taken on a guest tour still had to be considered. As a matter of fact, although a production might be given only once on a German stage, it could—by its frequent revivals during a tour—be marked out as worthy of note.

It is still more noteworthy that a scheduled performance was stopped on one occasion by a police ban. Not by an expressed one, which the high Dresden authorities would not have ventured against a sovereign theatre director related to the royal house—they would have found themselves in a peculiarly embarrassing position. But finally they deemed it their duty to inform the Lord Councillor Chronegk in unmistakable terms that this shocking and indecent play was not to be repeated. The Councillor dared not refuse this courteous wish and the sinister title *Ghosts* did not appear again on the theatre program. With the exception of Fitger and Lindner the Meininger had no luck with new authors, but on this occasion the fault did not lie in the selection of the play.[152] This work by Ibsen was given openly for the first time by the Meininger after it had been seen in Augsburg before a private audience under the sponsorship of Felix Phillipi.

The history of this work in Meiningen is not without humor. When it was readied for performance, a great agitation took possession of the little "Residenz." I do not believe that many of the Meininger—I mean here, naturally, the "sons of the soil"—had ever read *Ghosts;* but universal opinion held that the play was most indecent and immoral. Whether it was one or the other made no difference, because after all the two are the same; at any rate, such a play clearly did not belong on the stage.

Moreover, the feeling of the public was one of genuine irritation. We must realize, of course, that the Meininger were not really appreciated in their own home until they were no longer "The Meininger" and the guest tours had ceased. At the period of the guest engagements the repertoire was based entirely on plays prepared for the tours, and the plays scattered among them were frequently "bonbons," as the Duke was accustomed to say, which tasted better to him and his wife than to the public. Björnson's *Maria in Scotland* was a favorite play of this high-born gentleman and was given quite frequently. However, it enjoyed the general favor as little as *Lame Hulda* by the same author, for example, or Paul Heyse's plays.

This time, therefore, a determined protest was raised. That all the ladies would remain at home was certainly taken for granted; the subscription holders plotted a scandal; and that part of the public not holding subscriptions determined to show its disapproval and to display its courage by staying away. Therefore, almost no tickets were bought. This was unfortunate; the performance was to be given in Ibsen's presence, and the outstanding Berlin newspaper people were invited: Lindau, Landau, and

---

152When Ibsen's *Ghosts* appeared in 1881, many critics condemned it by declaring that a play dealing with the inherited effects of syphilis had no place on the public stage.

Weisstein. It was necessary to take immediate measures to counteract these schemes.

The Duke received knowledge of this bold conspiracy from my wife, whom he met while out walking.

"Well, are the people of Meiningen looking forward to enjoying themselves at *Ghosts?*" he had asked, and thereupon had to be told the exact opposite.

"We will have an empty house," my wife ended her report.

The Duke smiled, "It will be full as never before." And he predicted correctly—for he arranged to have the theatre seats given away. Anyone who would go to the office of the court marshal received tickets; and, in addition, all the court employees and court officials were ordered with friendly hints to be on hand in the theatre to applaud. As a guarantee against possible disturbances the entire police force of the "Residenz," to be sure only four or six men, was distributed about the auditorium.

The house was packed. Schiller's wish—theatre evenings for men only— was realized; with the exception of Frau von Heldburg only a few courageous women of the court theatre were present. The performance had a peaceful outcome; to be sure, the applause was bestowed only by the claque, the leader of whom was no less than His Highness, the Duke himself.

Afterwards, a large party was given at the castle. Ibsen appeared to be gratified; whether it was ever disclosed to him what a storm his "immoral" work had stirred up on the Werra, I have never found out. Characteristic was the answer which the Nordic poet gave to Weiser, who played Engstrand. When the actor asked whether the lame carpenter had set the asylum on fire—a point not made clear in the play—Ibsen seemed to consider earnestly for awhile and then answered: "That could be so." I received the impression that he spoke not of a figure of his own invention, but of a real person.

On July 1, 1890, in Odessa, the last performance of the guest engagements was given: *Twelfth Night,* a happy conclusion to a long, serious labor. The guest tours came to an end not because the interest of the public threatened to weaken, or because the Duke did not feel himself strong enough to go on; in most respects, the Meininger retired from the field in full strength. But the particular strength that had held the entire work together, the mainspring of the colossal clockwork, was growing weak. Chronegk had no longer been able to stand up under the physical and mental strains which this restless activity imposed. This man who seemed untiring, who knew no indulgence, finally broke down altogether.

It would have been possible to continue the management of the guest tours; the director, Paul Richard, an extremely intelligent and industrious man, had in the last years become Chronegk's right hand and had taken his place at different times with ability and skill. Although he was not animated by Chronegk's fiery zeal, he was still familiar with all the details of production. He then—as later, while Director of the Meininger Court Theatre—remained true to the Meininger tradition, even to the point of displaying too great pedantry at times. The Duke, however, felt himself too deeply indebted to Chronegk—that man who had made the Meininger his life work—to add to his pain by allowing him to see himself pushed aside by a successor.

Once I pressed the Duke to allow his company to prepare a farewell guest appearance in Berlin, one final look at the most successful productions, as one would usually crown a great edifice with a keystone. Also I did not fail to point out that one such farewell appearance of the Meininger could bring in to the theatre extraordinary revenue—capital for some future brilliant undertaking. After the old Duke had patiently listened to my long proposals, he interrupted our walk, stood still, and replied: "It is no longer necessary. What the German theatres had to learn, they have learned."

And that in fact was true. Throughout the decades they stand as testimony of the Meininger's influence.

Unceremoniously and quietly, without the great festive leave-taking which is so beloved in the theatre world, the Meininger came home again from their triumphal procession throughout the world to the little town on the Werra.

The originator of a great epoch of theatre history quietly and modestly departed from the stage; yet behind him there remained a firmly established path. Is it still perceptible today? Have the changing times failed to wipe it out?

CHAPTER XIV

THE IMPORTANCE OF THE MEININGER
FOR THE MODERN STAGE

I have already pointed out in the Preface that the modern stage has no single unifying style; that except for experiments rising here and there and then disappearing, it has for the most part two forms of presentation: the stylized and the expressionistic.[153] The scenic picture offered by both is basically different from that offered by the Meininger, who aimed only for illusion; indeed, at first glance it would seem that the Meininger were only a passing influence, with no hold on the theatre of today.

Nowadays historical truth is entirely ignored in the presentation of a dramatic work. Wallenstein, Don Philipp, and Götz move about in spaces which give no true representation of the locales in which they "lived." In historical plays we can, of course, still retain the costumes of a particular time, though without demanding scrupulous accuracy; and actresses have, as always, succeeded in adapting their costumes to the ruling fashion. Just as at one time they were able to smuggle the short waist, and then the crinoline, on to the stage, now they demand costumes which recognize the "modern line." In plays for which no definite time is prescribed by the author, the adaptation to period requirements in costuming is so slight that one could almost talk again about the introduction of a basic theatre costume.

Of course, costuming does have a wider variety than formerly—the result of the exuberant imagination of our painters and stage designers. A director no longer needs to trouble himself with the study of costume and art history; the artistic adviser designs the costumes and the scenery. The latter frequently gives his name to the inaccurate. In any case, he does not merely advise; he decides. In place of the abundance of color found in Meininger productions—which can be compared with the splendor of an oriental carpet, yet which in its gaiety usually produced a uniformity, we now aspire to a simpler and yet more grandiose color harmony.

This change in taste and in artistic point of view, however, does not affect the basic question, whether the stage has entirely abandoned the Meininger path. Also the fact that we now avoid battle scenes on the stage as often as possible is not under consideration here. When it is a question of real interdependence of the crowd with the movement of the play, as in *Caesar, Coriolanus,* and the concluding scenes of *Tell,* even today we

---
153Grube defines these terms in his Preface.

are hardly satisfied with mere hints; we still demand that supers reflect what is taking place between the principals. It is here that the Meininger model is so effective. The inspired direction of movement in the Meininger productions can no longer be ignored in the theatre world.

Adolf Winds suitably classified stage direction as "internal" and "external." What was mentioned above falls in the area of external direction; and with such changes even a pupil of the Meininger willingly comes to terms. If he is not entirely and pedantically bound to his master, incapable of conceiving any change, he will not fail to appreciate the great advantages which the external direction of today offers.

Meanwhile, if he casts a glance at the turn taken by internal direction, he faces a not always happy picture.

The star system—or its abuse—again raises its head, but still only in the capital city. The theatres elsewhere in the Republic hold themselves almost completely aloof from this system. In general, the custom of careful ensemble playing is standard; the regard given to the small—and even the smallest—parts is as great as that given by the Meininger. What difference does it make that one never thinks about how big a role the Meininger example played in restoring conscientiousness and industry to a somewhat debased stage?

The less meticulous attention that the setting now requires saves much time and allows a more searching and more careful attention to the poet's words than the Meininger could normally accord them. As an aftereffect of the naturalistic period, indistinct and slovenly speech is little by little being overcome. The newer poetic plays, relying more on meaning than on action, compel a careful use of speech.

On the other hand, even though the heritage of the Meininger has maintained itself in many respects—indeed has continued to grow—one of their basic principles seems to have been entirely lost: the regard, the reverence, which they dedicated to the poet. We live in a time of "interpretation," and the ambition of every director reaches its climax when he brings to the scenic interpretation something new, differing as much as possible from what has been done before. The living poet can oppose every such assault; often the director has to struggle with him about every cut, no matter how advantageous. But the classic poets can no longer defend themselves. In their plays anything that contradicts a given interpretation has been ruthlessly struck out. Some directors have departed so far from the costume accuracy of the Meininger that they have presented classical pieces in modern dress, even in theatres of considerable reputation: in the Hamburg Little Theatre production of *The Robbers,* and in *Clavigo*[154] at the Oldenburg Landestheater. Goethe's tragedy ends, as we know, with a duel of the hero and Beaumarchais. Nowadays, we are not accustomed to walk about with swords at our sides, so here the director was faced

154*Clavigo* (1774), Goethe's middle-class tragedy.

with a difficulty. But he knew how to overcome it; he allowed Beaumarchais to draw a revolver and simply shoot his enemy down. At another great theatre we have seen *Fiesko* performed without properties; therefore, just as the actor has to improvise for himself at a rehearsal—though he ought never to have to do so—the actor in *Fiesko* reads letters from his open hand, throws about gold from a non-existent purse, stabs someone with a clenched fist, etc.

Those are abuses, bubbles which the exuberant spirit of young directors have whipped up and at which in later years they will smile; but—to change the figure—is the soil that can produce such plants a thoroughly healthy one? And how do more important matters fare—the textual adaptations in which our great works appear before us?

When scarcely half of *Wallenstein's Camp* is performed; when Max and Thekla are reduced through ruthless cutting to subordinate figures (even though they represent a counterpoint to the egotism which moves all the other characters); when Melchthal's wonderful observations on the light of the eyes—observations arising from the deepest grief—fall to the red pencil, then it is as though we were to cut away the full flesh in order to bring the bone structure into sharper relief. When well-known and long-familiar selections are omitted (perhaps only because they are so), there is a meager compensation for the loss of so much poetical wealth: other selections, previously considered unimportant, are brought to the attention of the audience. Occasionally it appears that such cuts are made only to introduce something new. It is gratifying that there has been an effort to bring Shakespeare to the stage with as few cuts and changes as possible—why won't directors allow our German classics the same right? Is such an assault on our masterpieces called honoring our masters?

But let us turn back again to external direction. Certain devices—which to be sure the Meininger did not invent, but did develop—are still of value now.

The importance of sound-effects on stage and especially behind the scenes—how much they added to an effect, to increase a mood, to produce an illusion, or, as one is accustomed to say today, to elevate the activity of the imagination—was first taught by the Meininger. The earlier discussions of *Wallenstein* or *The Ancestress* will emphasize this point for the reader.

If today every better-class theatre has a director of music, here, too, is a reminder of the Meininger. Once the theatre had a certain number of fanfares and marches, and these always reoccurred in a regular series! Occasionally in the great art centers, plays would be "set to music" as people jokingly put it in those days, to provide melodramas and other plays of that sort with between-act music. The Leipzig director of the orchestra, Mühldorfer, had brought himself a certain amount of fame on the basis of his compositions for Shakespeare's plays, which Haase included in his productions according to Kean's example. In general, we then thought little of introducing music suitable to the action as well as to the characterizations of the play, let alone of writing a special composition for such a purpose. The extremely skillful musical director of the Meiningen Theatre, Reiff, deserves mention here as the prototype of all stage musical directors. He had notable skill in arranging the instrumentation of older musical motifs in a uniquely archaic effect.

That even the artistic adviser, the scene painter, is no longer a mere assistant—i.e., once the Duke had produced picturesque effects of a sort previously unknown—has already been mentioned.

To introduce still another point: the Meininger freed the stage from the monotony of the never-varying rectangular setting. Before the Duke's time, the rectangular arrangement was seldom altered, and then only when absolutely necessary; little attempt was ever made to produce a picturesque impression by varying the shape. An interior with a balcony, with angled corners, or even with a diagonal wall was unknown. Little consideration was ever given to providing a more charming arrangement of streets and squares by setting houses, gates, fountains, and items of that kind out from the usual rows of wings. We all had to satisfy ourselves with a backdrop on which buildings were painted and with stock wings which were pushed toward the center of the stage. The stage rectangle remained unchanged.

The Meininger never pushed the wings (which were a legacy from the Rococo theatre) farther on stage, but rather pushed them offstage. They did not invent the box setting, as was frequently supposed. This error was correctly refuted by Adolf Winds, who could have alluded to the fact that Diderot in an article in his *Encyclopedia*[155] wished for the appearance of just such a "chamber." On the other hand, the Meininger did contribute very much to its adoption. The advantages which a closed box set brings to a realistic performance are still retained by the stylized theatre; only the expressionistic[156] theatres are willing to return to the unreality of wings and hanging drops.

The Meininger also first undertook to break up the flatness of the stage floor with steps and levels. Before their time we employed these only when there was an urgent necessity; as decorative elements and as a necessary principle of presentation they were rarely considered, even though as early as 1858, Dingelstedt, in his "Studies" for his production of *The Bride of Messina,* for example, had proposed the use of levels. That the step unit has now become almost a holy symbol is certainly common knowledge.

Dingelstedt must be considered a forerunner of the Meininger in his approach to the picturesque as well. But anyone who had the opportunity to see his productions before he in turn came under the influence of the Meininger knows that his stage "decorations," as their very name implies, were not much more than "embellishments," as they were called in the eighteenth century. The plays he directed later were entirely different. One

---

155Denis Diderot (1713-84) became editor of the *Encyclopedia* in 1747.
156For Grube's definitions of "stylized" and "expressionistic" see his Preface.

of his most outstanding was *Woe to Him Who Lies*.[157] Next to this his formerly much-praised production of *The Winter's Tale* seems somewhat dull.

Grillparzer's comedy, which at one time had been shamefully neglected, was restored to popularity by this great Viennese theatre man.[158] Its subsequent success may in no small part be ascribed to his lively and humorous production. Dingelstedt did not, as did many, sink under the weight of the Meininger method; he took the spirit of the Meininger and made it his own. By utilizing all the expedients of the stage, he knew how to bring out technical ability as well as artistry in the actors.

Indeed, the distinguishing mark of a great work of art is that it appears to us an absolute necessity just as it is, that the magic with which it surrounds us does not permit us to think that it could ever be otherwise. The great advantage which the art of theatre enjoys over other arts lies in the fact that it constantly practices this magic. Nowadays we may criticize the details of a performance adversely, but we are so accustomed to the fact that the director, the actors, and the designers strive in the closest unity toward an objective set by the director that we cannot imagine it was ever any different. Only a few who can remember a time before the Meininger realize that this unity did not always exist.

At that time the actor was a jewel blazing on a dark velvet background; now the stone is artistically mounted, part of a piece of jewelry. At that time the *Régisseur* was nothing more than a "monitor," as he was known in the eighteenth century; for the first time the Meininger made him a "director."[159]

Adolf Winds opposed this German title, which he said did not express the manifold obligations of the office. Well, language does not always proceed logically when it coins or admits new words; life is not insured by life insurance; the telephone does not speak and the receiver does not hear.[160] Perhaps *Spielmeister* or *Spielführer* would be more nearly correct, but commander-in-chief and supreme commander seem to me synonymous, and with the German word one can still imagine more than with the foreign word, *régie,* which originally signified merely management. Therefore, let us hold to the Meininger creation, "director." For the director, they converted a disorderly state into a realm which is subject to one resolute, sovereign will.

Changes in prevailing fashion, in artistic interpretation, in points of view about what is beautiful will always appear; no trend, indeed no style, is preserved forever, but from each somehow something survives which later times accept, use, or develop more fully.

157 Grillparzer's only comedy (1840).
158 *i.e.,* Dingelstedt.
159 The German word for "director" used by Grube is *Spielleiter,* a "play leader."
160 This is a play on German words which does not lend itself to translation: the German word for telephone is *fernsprecher,* a "distant speaker," and the word for receiver is *hörer,* a "hearer."

The stage not merely as a base and background of the theatrical performance: the stage as a complete work of art! That is the central idea the Meininger were first to proclaim. Its realization was the achievement which secured for the artist, Duke Georg, a perpetual place of honor in the history of the theatre.

THE GUEST PERFORMANCES OF THE MEININGER — FIRST TABLE

City	Julius Caesar	Pope Sixtus V	Twelfth Night	Massacre of St. Bartholomew	Between the Battles	Imaginary Invalid	Merchant of Venice	Battle of Arminius	Esther	The Learned Ladies	Fiesko	Kathy of Heilbronn	Hereditary Forester	William Tell	The Pretenders	Macbeth	The Robbers	Prince of Homburg	The Winter's Tale	The Ancestress	Wallenstein's Camp	Iphigenia in Tauris	Preciosa	Taming of the Shrew	Piccolomini	Wallenstein's Death	The Witch	Lydia	The Crucifx Carver	Maria Stuart	Miss Sara Sampson	Bride of Messina	Marino Faliero	The Maid of Orleans	The Great Galeoto	Alexandra	Ghosts	Rose of Tyburn	Frau Lucrezia	's Nullel!
Berlin	52		6	11	6	11	5	15	15	10	29	16	2	21	7	5	13	10	27	6	6	24	1	6	24	21	13			9		3	3	3						
Vienna	16		7	6	4	6	5	17	6	3	7	4	1	10	8		5	7	10	10	6	6	4	4	6	6	7	5	3	8		3	3	55	3	2				
Budapest	9		6	11	1	6	5	4	6	1	5	2		10	8		2	4	9	4	7	7	3	3	6	3	10	2	3	8		2		5	5	2	1			
Dresden	10		11	9	5	6	8	10	6		9	10		7	7		4	4	17	7	16			3	6	7	10	2		10		2	2	13	3	2	1			
Breslau	35		20	3	12	12	8	10	10	3	18	10	5	19	7		8	2	7	2	16	4	8	6	12	10	10	2	2	10			2	14	1	3	1	2		
Cologne	14		5	3	3	3	3		3		12	6		12			5	3	14		6		3	3	6	4	3						3							
Frankfurt/Main	8		3	2	3	3	6	4	3	1	4	4		3			8	3	11	5	8	2	5		4	3														
Prague	10		5	7	1	3		8	2	2	12	7		11			6	3	5	2	8				5	4			2	3				5						
Leipzig	19		5	1	1	3	4	8	7	3	4	4		9			8	3	11		6	1			6	5			2	10			1	11						
Hamburg	4		10	8	2	3	4	4	2	1	5	5		5			3	2	5	1	2	2			7	2			2	3		2	2							
Amsterdam	6		3	3	2	2	4		3	2	6	6		7			6	3	5		3				6	4	3			4			1	10	3	3			2	1
Duesseldorf	11		4	3	2	2	3		3	2	6	5		5			4	3	5	1	6		3		4	3				4		2		10	11	3				
Graz	11		5	1	1	2	4				6	4		7			4	2	5		2				7	4		2	2	5		1	2	11	9					
Bremen	7		6	1		2	3				4	4		6			4		11	1	2	2			6	5	3		1	3		1	1	5	5					
London	16		3	2	1	1	4				1	3		8			3	2	6	1	2	1	3		3	5	2			4			1							
Nüernberg	4		3	2	2	2			2		2	3		5			2		7		2		2		6	2			2	2			2							
Barmen	6		1				4				2			4				2	5		3	1			6	5	3	2		3										
Magdeburg	4		3			2	4			2	2	3		5			2		6	1	6	2			4	2	1			4		1								
Munich	7		2	1	1	2	4				2	3		4			3	2	5	3	7		2		7	3	1		1	2										
Mainz	7		1	1	2	4	4				3	3		7			3		6	2	6				6	2	2			3										
Strasbourg, Baden, Metz	6		4			4	3			3	3	3		9			3	2	4	1	7				6	2				3			2							
Basel	10		3			1	4				2	2		6			3		3	3	7				6	2		2		4			1							
St. Petersburg	12		1			1	3				3	3		3			2		4	2	7	1	3		3	2				4			2							
Moscow	7		5			1	4				1			4			2		3		3				3	2		3		5			1							
Warsaw	4		3	1	1	1	3				4	4		4			2		4	3	3		2		3	2		1		3										
Königsberg	4		1	1			4				3	3		4			3		4	2	4	1			3	2		1		4										
Trieste	4		2			3					3	3		4			2		3	1	6			3	3	3				3				7						
Antwerp	3		3			2	3			2	3	3		3			3		4	2	6				3	3				3				6				1		
Rotterdam	4		3				4				3	3		4					4	1	6				3	2				4		1	2	5						
Brussels	3		1			1	3					3		3			3		3		6				2	2		2		4			1	7						
Gotha	1										1	1																												
Stettin	4		3	2		3	3							3			3	3	4		3				3	2	2	4	2	4			2	5		5				
Copenhagen	3		3	1	1	1	4	3	1		1	3		2			1		3		3		3		3	2		3	1	3			1	6		6	1			
Stockholm	4		1	2		2	1				4	4		4					2		4				3	1		1	2	4		2		2		7				
Kiev	2		2			1	2			1	1	2		3			1		3		2		1		3	1				3		1				2				
Odessa	3		3	3		2	4			1	2	3		3			1		3		2	1	3		2	2	2	1	2	4		2	1	4	2			1	2	2
Total	330	4	132	85	21	83	94	101	74	29	152	83	7	223	10	2	104	38	233	79	176	14	54	21	161	140	56	25	11	89	7	11	19	194	7	5	2	5	2	2

THE GUEST APPEARANCES OF THE MEININGER — SECOND TABLE

	1874	1875	1876	1877	1878	1879	1880	1881	1882	1883	1884	1885	1886	1887	1888	1889	1890	Number Of Appearances
Berlin	47	60	48	—	46	—	—	—	78	—	43	—	—	63	—	—	—	385
Vienna	—	37	—	—	—	—	—	—	—	35	—	—	—	—	40	—	—	112
Budapest	—	17	25	26	—	23	—	—	—	—	—	—	—	—	—	—	—	99
Dresden	—	—	33	39	32	—	—	—	—	—	—	—	—	35	—	—	—	164
Breslau	—	—	—	41	20	34	32	31	33	25	29	—	24	—	—	—	—	269
Cologne	—	—	—	24	27	—	—	—	—	—	—	—	—	—	—	—	—	75
Frankfurt/Main	—	—	—	—	32	31	—	—	—	—	—	—	—	—	—	—	—	44
Prague	—	—	—	—	—	39	40	—	21	—	—	—	—	—	—	—	—	110
Leipzig	—	—	—	—	—	40	—	—	—	25	—	—	—	31	35	—	—	159
Hamburg	—	—	—	—	—	39	—	—	—	—	—	—	—	—	—	—	—	39
Amsterdam	—	—	—	—	—	—	39	—	—	—	—	—	—	—	—	—	—	39
Duesseldorf	—	—	—	—	—	—	48	32	—	—	—	—	—	—	—	—	—	82
Graz	—	—	—	—	—	—	32	30	29	—	—	—	—	—	—	—	—	108
Bremen	—	—	—	—	—	—	26	28	26	—	—	—	—	—	—	—	—	54
London	—	—	—	—	—	—	56	—	—	—	—	—	—	—	—	—	—	56
Nuernberg	—	—	—	—	—	—	—	—	29	—	—	—	—	—	—	—	—	29
Barmen	—	—	—	—	—	—	—	—	—	26	—	—	24	—	—	—	—	50
Magdeburg	—	—	—	—	—	—	—	—	—	27	—	—	—	—	—	—	—	27
Munich	—	—	—	—	—	—	—	—	—	31	28	—	—	—	—	—	—	59
Mainz	—	—	—	—	—	—	—	—	—	—	28	—	28	—	—	—	—	56
Strasbourg, Baden, Metz	—	—	—	—	—	—	—	—	—	—	34	—	31	—	—	—	—	65
Basel	—	—	—	—	—	—	—	—	—	—	28	—	—	45	—	—	—	73
St. Petersburg	—	—	—	—	—	—	—	—	—	—	—	39	—	—	38	—	—	77
Moscow	—	—	—	—	—	—	—	—	—	—	—	29	—	—	28	—	—	57
Warsaw	—	—	—	—	—	—	—	—	—	—	—	24	—	—	—	—	—	24
Königsberg	—	—	—	—	—	—	—	—	—	—	—	29	—	—	—	—	—	29
Trieste	—	—	—	—	—	—	—	—	—	—	—	29	—	—	—	—	—	29
Antwerp	—	—	—	—	—	—	—	—	—	—	—	—	—	—	29	—	—	29
Rotterdam	—	—	—	—	—	—	—	—	—	—	—	—	—	—	30	—	—	30
Brussels	—	—	—	—	—	—	—	—	—	—	—	—	—	—	29	—	—	29
Gotha	—	—	—	—	—	—	—	—	—	—	—	—	—	—	—	2	—	2
Stettin	—	—	—	—	—	—	—	—	—	—	—	—	—	—	—	27	—	27
Copenhagen	—	—	—	—	—	—	—	—	—	—	—	—	—	—	—	30	—	30
Stockholm	—	—	—	—	—	—	—	—	—	—	—	—	—	—	—	30	—	30
Kiev	—	—	—	—	—	—	—	—	—	—	—	—	—	—	—	—	14	14
Odessa	—	—	—	—	—	—	—	—	—	—	—	—	—	—	—	—	30	30
Number Of Appearances During Each Year	47	114	106	130	157	167	159	172	182	202	196	178	86	235	194	156	110	2591

Number of Performances in the Individual Cities

Berlin	385	in 8	Appearances
Breslau	269	in 8	Appearances
Dresden	164	in 6	Appearances
Leipzig	159	in 5	Appearances
Vienna	112	in 3	Appearances
Prague	110	in 4	Appearances
Graz	108	in 4	Appearances
Budapest	99	in 4	Appearances
Duesseldorf	82	in 2	Appearances
St. Petersburg	77	in 2	Appearances
Cologne	75	in 2	Appearances
Basel	73	in 2	Appearances
Strasbourg	65	in 2	Appearances
Munich	59	in 2	Appearances
Moscow	57	in 2	Appearances
London	56	in 1	Appearance
Mainz	56	in 2	Appearances
Bremen	54	in 2	Appearances
Barmen	50	in 2	Appearances
Frankfurt/Main	44	in 2	Appearances
Hamburg	39	in 1	Appearance
Amsterdam	39	in 1	Appearance
Rotterdam	30	in 1	Appearance
Copenhagen	30	in 1	Appearance
Stockholm	30	in 1	Appearance
Odessa	30	in 1	Appearance
Nuernberg	29	in 1	Appearance
Königsberg	29	in 1	Appearance
Trieste	29	in 1	Appearance
Antwerp	29	in 1	Appearance
Brussels	29	in 1	Appearance
Magdeburg	27	in 1	Appearance
Stettin	27	in 1	Appearance
Warsaw	24	in 1	Appearance
Kiev	14	in 1	Appearance
Gotha	2	in 1	Appearance
	2591	in 81	Appearances

LIST OF PLATES

*The plates follow; in each case credits are
given in the accompanying captions.*

PLATE I—Duke Georg II in 1912.
Drawing by his son, Prince Ernst.
(Geschichte der Meininger)

PLATE II—Helene von Heldburg.
Painting by Franz von Lenbach.
(Geschichte der Meininger)

PLATE III A—Ludwig Chronegk in 1887.
(Meininger Museum)

PLATE III B—Chronegk with his bell, directing the rehearsal
of the Battle of Philippi in *Julius Caesar*. Drawing by C. W.
Allers. (Cologne Theatre Museum)

PLATE IV A—Antony's oration in *Julius Caesar,* 1874. Drawing
by J. Kleinmichel based on a sketch by Duke Georg II.
(Cologne Theatre Museum)

PLATE IV B—Landscape from *Six Drawings by Duke Georg II.*
(Cologne Theatre Museum)

PLATE V A—Max Grube, as Talbot in his death scene from *The Maid of Orleans,* leaning against a stuffed horse. (Meininger Museum)

PLATE V B—Sketch by Duke Georg II showing in the lower left hand corner a stuffed horse in a scene for *The Battle of Arminius.*
(Geschichte der Meininger)

PLATE VI A—Ludwig Barnay as Marc Antony in
Julius Caesar, 1874. (Meininger Museum)

PLATE VI B— *Wallenstein* costumes designed
by Duke Georg II. Drawing by C. W. Allers.
(Cologne Theatre Museum)

PLATE VII A—Josef Weilenbeck as
Argan in *The Imaginary Invalid*, 1874.
(Meininger Museum)

PLATE VII B—Final scene of *The Battle of Arminius*, 1875.
Drawing by Hugo Ströhl of the Vienna performance.
(Cologne Theatre Museum)

PLATE VIII A—Roman soldier carrying authentic pack, shovel, and javelin. Drawing by Duke Georg II for *The Battle of Arminius*. (Meininger Museum)

PLATE VIII B—Appearance of Alraune in *The Battle of Arminius* showing fallen tree obstructing the narrow path. Pen and ink sketch by Duke Georg II. (Meininger Museum)

PLATE IX A—Storming of St. Thomas' Gate in *Fiesko*, 1875.
(Geschichte der Meininger)

PLATE IX B—Josef Nesper as *Fiesko*, 1875.
(Meininger Museum)

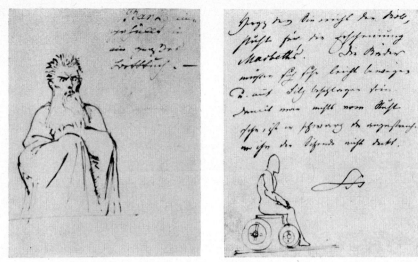

PLATE X A—Sketch for Banquo's ghost and wagon for rolling it into banquet scene in *Macbeth*, 1886. Pen and ink sketches by Duke Georg II. (Cologne Theatre Museum)

PLATE X B—Design for banquet scene in *Macbeth*. Entrance trap for murderer down right. Pen and ink sketch by Duke Georg II. *(Geschichte der Meininger)*

PLATE XI A—Karl Weiser as Franz Moor and Auguste Prasch-Grevenberg as Amalia in *The Robbers*, 1878. Eighteenth-century costumes designed by Duke Georg II. Drawing by C. W. Allers. (Cologne Theatre Museum)

PLATE XI B—Costume design for "Old Man Moor" in the "Hunger Tower" scene of *The Robbers*. Drawing by Duke Georg II. (Meininger Museum)

PLATE XII A—Setting for the battle of Fehrbellin in *The Prince of Homburg*, 1878. Holes were punched in the backdrop for the insertion of fire crackers in an effort to simulate distant gunfire. Pen and pencil sketch by Duke Georg II. (Meininger Museum)

PLATE XII B—Marie von Moser-Sperner as Berta and Paul Richard as Count Borotin in *The Ancestress*, 1878. (Meininger Museum)

PLATE XIII A—The "iron sea" of von Pappenheim's cavalry in *Wallenstein's Death*, 1882. All of the cavalry men are costumed in the correct "blackened breastplate." Drawing by Julius Ehrentraut from *Illustrierte Frauen-Zeitung*. (Cologne Theatre Museum)

PLATE XIII B—Emma Teller-Habelmann as Elizabeth in *Maria Stuart*. (Cologne Theatre Museum)

PLATE XIV A—Elizabeth's throne room in *Maria Stuart,* Act II, 1882.
(Geschichte der Meininger)

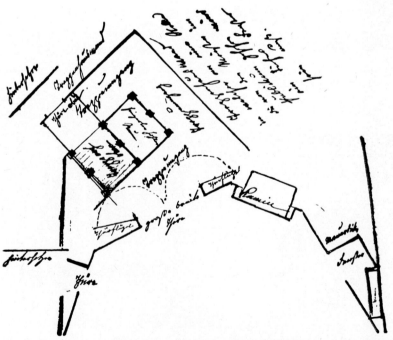

PLATE XIV B—Ground plan of final scene of *Maria Stuart* showing double doors and stairway. Drawing by Duke Georg II. *(Geschichte der Meininger)*

PLATE XV A—Amanda Lindner as *The Maid of Orleans,*
1890. Drawing by C. W. Allers. (Cologne Theatre Museum)

PLATE XV B—Final design for the prologue in *The Maid of
Orleans* with the chapel right foreground and the magic oak center.
Drawing by Duke Georg II. *(Geschichte der Meininger)*

PLATE XVI A—Preparations for the coronation scene in *The Maid of Orleans*. At center, Ruprecht, the property master, enters with hand properties. At right the costume masters Schwencke and Geisenhöner. Drawing by C. W. Allers. (Cologne Theatre Museum)

PLATE XVI B—Coronation scene in *The Maid of Orleans*. In order to suggest a huge crowd only the central door of Rheims cathedral was shown. In earlier productions the entire facade of the cathedral had been painted on a backdrop. Pencil drawing by Duke Georg II. (Meininger Museum)